# Voice of the Innocent

# Voice of the Innocent

A plead for justice knowing
that it could happen to you

# Emmett K. Shasha

**To order additional copies of this book, contact:**
Xlibris Corporation
1-888-795-4274
www.Xlibris.com
Orders@Xlibris.com
121708

# TABLE OF CONTENTS

# PREFACE

I have earlier asked two persons to read my manuscript and then write the preface of this book. But because of their huge obligations, they were unable to contribute to my work. Knowing the subject matter intimately, I decided to write the preface myself. There are many proverbs that are sometimes quoted by people of goodwill. They sometimes do the quoting, but in actual life, they are not touched by the proverb which they quote. If I said, "When a chicken is white, it is white," meaning that if a man is innocent, no matter what, where you took him or what you did, in the end you will find out that he is innocent.

There are those who call themselves Christians, but with the exception of a few, the broad majorities read the scripture without fully understanding the scripture. To understand the Scripture, one must live the Scripture every day of their lives. That is accomplished by applying and living the words of Christ daily.

Joseph, son of Jacob, son of Isaac, the son of Abraham, is one name which is mentioned time and again in this book. Mentioned not in the time of his glory but in the time of his worse circumstance. I chose to identify myself with this biblical character to tell the story of my innocence. I also employed another biblical character with whom I also chose to identify myself, that is righteous Job of the East. I am identifying with this biblical character not in his glory but during his worse circumstance. Why did I choose Job? Like Joseph, to prove my innocence, I chose Job to prove that it is not for any sin I committed that brought upon me this temptation. That's why I asked the question, "Is it destiny?"

Remember this scripture from St. John 9:2-3, "*And his disciples asked him, saying, Master, who did sin, this man, or his parents, that he was born blind? Jesus answered, Neither hath this man sinned, nor his parents: but that the work of God should be made manifest in him*" (Holy Bible, KJV). Again, I tell my story with spiritual implication. There are those who just don't believe in anything like dreams or visions. Some of these very people are Christians. Let me give two occasions here, one taken from the Old Testaments and the other taken from the New Testament. The OT account: Solomon had just become king of Israel, after the death of his father David. Being the person he was at the time, upon his enthronement, Solomon made a request to God (1 Kings 3:9), "*Give therefore thy servant an understanding heart to judge thy people, that I may discern between good and bad.*"

The scripture then goes on to tell us that the request of Solomon pleased the Lord and he responded by saying (see verse 12a of the same chapter), "*Behold, I have done according to thy words lo I have given thee a wise and an understanding heart."* Something very interesting takes place in verse 15. *"And Solomon awoke; and, behold, it was a dream"* (Holy Bible, KJV). He asked physically, he received an answer spiritually. The manifestations to his request took place physically.

For those of you that are Bible scholars know how great Solomon became. James 4:2b says, *"Yet ye have not, because ye ask not."* Jesus said in St. Matthew 7:7, *"Ask, and it shall be given you; see, and ye shall find; knock, and it shall be opened unto you,"* (Holy Bible, KJV). So it is in asking that one receives. I tell that I wanted to know. I then devoted myself in prayers. As I did, I then began to ask questions and I got answers spiritually and physically.

On the other hand, if the hand of the Lord is upon you, sometimes you really don't have to ask for information. He will just give it to you for his glory. From the Scripture, we also see in the NT where a believer and a disciple received a revelation that they did not ask for. Acts 10:3-5 says, *"He saw in a vision evidently about the ninth hour of the day an angel of God coming in to him, and saying unto him Cornelius. And when he looked on him, he was afraid, and he said unto him, Thy prayers and thine alms are come up for a memorial before God. And now send men to Joppa, and call for one Simon, whose surname is Peter."*

In response to Cornelius's vision, see what takes place in verses 9-20 of the same chapter. *"On the morrow, as they went on their journey, and drew nigh unto the city, Peter went up upon the house top to pray about the six hour . . . he fell into a trance. And saw heaven opened . . . And there came a voice to him . . . And the voice spake unto him again the second time . . . This was done thrice: and the vessel was received up again into heaven . . . Peter doubted in himself what this vision which he had seen should mean, behold, the men which were sent from Cornelius had made enquiry for Simon's house . . . and asked whether Simon, which was surname Peter, were lodged there. While Peter thought on the vision, the Spirit said unto him Behold, three men seek thee. Arise therefore, and get thee down, and go with them, doubting nothing: for I have sent them"* Holy Bible (KJV)

*"I will pour out of my Spirit upon all flesh: and your son and your daughters shall prophesy, and your young men shall see vision, and your old men shall dream dreams"* (Acts 2:17).

What you just read is exactly how I obtained the information I was given to tell of my plight: the temptations that have come upon me in this land. By the time you are done reading this book, perhaps you too might be inspired to obtain information from the spiritual realm. Let me say that if it is not unto a godly intent, don't engage. It could lead to your demise.

Proverbs 16:25 says, *"There is a way that seemeth right unto a man, but the end thereof are the ways of death"* (Holy Bible, KJV). But if you seek to know the true source of the matter, as you devote yourselves to the glory of God, you shall receive. In so doing, let this be your attitude. Psalms 1:1-2: *"Blessed is the man that walketh not in the counsel of the ungodly, nor standeth in the way of sinners . . . But his delight is in the law of the LORD; and in his law doth he meditate day and night"* (Holy Bible, KJV).

The story of my life, as recorded here in this book, is true. Even the God of my fathers who had substance me and also testified of me unto his servant Rev. Ivan E. B. Pittman, saying, "The Lord says that you are an honest man." Is my witness.

With the publishing of this book rather than handing out insults at the author for the board step taken; because of his birth origin, to increase what is already in place against his life, I believe that the author be allow to live in peace having a peace of mind.

A word of wisdom: "When they were but a few men in number; yea, very few, and strangers in it. When they went from one nation to another, from one kingdom to another people; He suffered no man to do them wrong: yea he reproved kings for their sakes; Saying. Touch not mine anointed, and do my prophets no harm."

If you are still in doubt that accessing information from the spirit realm is impossible, ask Sir Roth, host of *It's Supernatural.* He will tell you of the experiences of many of his guests.

# ACKNOWLEDGEMENT

In writing this acknowledgement, I will commence it with the verses of Psalms 107:1-2, which says, *"Oh give thanks unto the LORD, for he is good: for his mercy enduredth for ever. Let the redeemed of the LORD say so, whom he hath redeem from the hand of the enemy."*

When this plight started, before going to the Lord in prayers to ask questions, I thought that it was one of those headaches that would come upon you and you will only have to take a pain tablet, and the headache would be gone. Because of that, I did my usual prayers for strength and sat down.

When I noticed that the plight was not going away, I began to get concerned as I did my next step, was to go to the place of safety. Once there, I could then begin to ask questions.

My place of safety comes from here: *"He that dwelleth in the secret place of the most High shall abide under the shadow of the Almighty . . . For he shall give his angels charge over thee, to keep thee in all thy ways. They shall bear thee up in their hands, lest thou dash thy foot against a stone"* (Psalms 91:1, 11-12). While safely resting beneath the shadow of the Almighty, I then began to cry unto him.

*"In my distress I called upon the LORD, and cried unto my God: he heard my voice out of his temple, and my cry came before him, even into his ears"* (Psalms 18:6). As I poured out my heart to God in tears, this then became my meditation, *"The righteous cry, and the LORD heareth, and delivereth them out of all their troubles. The LORD is nigh unto them that are of a broken heart; and saveth such as be of a contrite spirit. Many are the affliction of the righteous: but the LORD delivereth him out of them all"* (Psalms 34:17-19). Having these sureties, I could then process to inquire spiritually and await the physical manifestation.

I commence my inquiry with a deep sense of devotion in prayers to the Lord, asking him for both spiritual and physical revelation. I also asked the Lord for protection from harm and danger and to deliver me from shame and disgrace. I made mention of the three angels' visitation, who held in their hands what look like a curtain. They held it about shoulder length around me; then one of them spoke to me and said, "No shame or disgrace will come to any one." I didn't understand then, but I do now. By then I was saying to myself, I have done harm to no one. I have done wrong to no one. I am not doing drugs, nor am I following someone's wife. Why? Why is this happening I need to know the answers. It was not long after that I began receiving revelations and answers.

I spoke of angelic visitation that was in 2003. One thing I didn't do was to ask them for their names. This visitation was not the first. The first time I got a visit from the angels was in 1995. We were at the church (Children of Salvation the Ark) going through a three days' dry fast. When they came, they were three in number. What they told me I have shared with no man, not even my wife, because the time is not appropriate. But I did ask for the name of the one that spoke with me. "Why do you want to know my name?" he asked as they walk away.

I am very grateful to God through his Son Jesus Christ for keeping his word to me. I blessed God also for my wife Laverne Y. Shasha, who gives me the liberty to spend time in the basement of our home there in my office to write. I bless God for the children; they did their best keeping tranquility in our home while I was writing. I also bless God for little Desire, my granddaughter (Su-pi-su-pi, baby's nickname). She's three years old. She will do everything to get my attention; if it meant that I will have to stop writing, then so be it. Because for her, she considers our time together to be everything.

I am grateful to God for the families of Sound Doctrine Baptist Fellowship International. I say thanks to you all for staying and standing with me in the church. Like the many that left, you too could have gone, but you chose to stay. I say thanks.

Special thanks to my pastor and mentors Pastor Paul M. Gabriel. Thanks to the families of Cross Road Baptist Church who have allowed our church to use their facilities without charge. Thanks.

Thanks to Mrs. Shionah Woodtor Chanallor, a dear sister, for her encouragement to get me to start writing. Even though I didn't start with her topic of interest, which is "spiritual warfare and deliverance," it is my hope that when I do write that book, I will dedicate it to her.

Special thanks to you, the general public, for your concern in wanting to listen to what I have to share with you. Thanks.

Thanks to all those that will stand up for justice and human rights. Remember, today it is Emmett, tomorrow it could be you.

As you are about to read this book, when you come to the end, before making any comment be it for or against me, let these words of knowledge be your guide: *"And I saw the dead, small and great, stand before God; and the books were open: and another book was open, which is the book of life: and the dead were judge out of those things which were written in the books, according to their works. And the sea gave up the dead which were in it; and death and hell delivered up the dead which were in them: and they were judged every man according to their works. And death and hell were cast into the lake of fire. This is the second death. And whosoever was not found written in the book of life was cast into the lake of fire"* Revelation 20:12-15

# Knowing the Author

I will introduce myself later on in my writing; for now, I just want the world to know me before meeting me. Why this format? one may ask; well, that is how many people get to know people. And without a former introduction, conclusions are drawn. It is in an introduction that acquaintances are made. But the society in which we now live it is not so now and days.

As you read about my life, there are many things that you will identify with; some you will comprehend, others will be mind-boggling and some of which will be very much upsetting to you. When you are done, you will be at liberty to draw a conclusion; perhaps just like me, you will want some answers. Maybe it is by you or with your help that we can together seek justice for the needy.

Having commenced the reading of this book, I urge you to sit attentively and contemplate on every sentence so that you can get the best out of your reading.

I read the book of Genesis of the Holy Bible many times before, but I did not become so obsessed with the story of Joseph, until the same thing that happened to him began happening to me, but in a different manner.

Unlike Joseph who went to prison, no law enforcement officer had approached me or questioned me concerning the temptation, which came upon me in this land. While it is true that no law enforcement officer had ever questioned me or taken me to court, I have already been found guilty by the public.

Talk about character assassination and the drawing of one's name in the mud. That is exactly what I am enduring even as I commence the writing of this book on April 15, 2012.

If I had not been questioned by a law enforcement personnel, taken to court, or put in prison, how then did I get to know what I am about to share with the public? Well, I urge you to open your eyes to see. Going through the narrative, you will notice both the physical and the spiritual realm playing out.

I do not profess to be a prophet, but I have in me the spirit of righteousness. Which give me access to my Heavenly Father. In the Old Testaments book of Numbers chapter 12 verses 5-8, God said something very interesting, "*And the LORD came down in the pillar of the cloud, and stood in the door of the tabernacle, and called Aaron and Miriam: and they both came forth. And he said, Hear now my words: If there be a prophet among you, I the LORD will make myself known unto him in a vision, and will speak unto him in a dream. My servant Moses is not so, who is faithful in all mine house. With him will I speak mouth to mouth, even apparently, and not in dark speeches"* (Holy Bible, KJV).

Because of this, I came to realize that as the Lord worked with the prophet of old, he is still doing the same thing even today.

A Syrian officer testified saying *"None, my lord, O King: but Elisha, the prophet that is in Israel, telleth the king of Israel the words that thou speakest in thy bedchamber"* (Holy Bible, KJV).

While he had not yet appeared unto me physically as he did with his servant Moses? I have been blessed to hear him speak to me openly. He had also spoken to me from my heart, in dreams and visions. I have also been blessed to have seen him spiritually.

The blessing of hearing him speak to me has saved my life on many occasions; it had also made me aware of my surroundings in terms of imminent danger. I will give a background on how it all started. After which, I will tell the similarity of the plight of Joseph's life in Egypt, as recorded in Genesis 39, and that of my life here in the United States of America. In the end, you will have the option to judge for yourselves.

## Hearing from God

I should have graduated from the twelfth grade in 1985, from the Robertsport Government High School in Robertsport Grand Cape Mount County, Liberia. But before marching, one had to successfully pass in both the school and the West African Examination (WAEC).

I successfully passed the school exam but not the WAEC. I failed two subjects: science and math. I reset for both subjects in 1986, this time around, I passed science and again failed at math. I again reregistered to sit for math in 1987, this time I was very determined to pass. By then I had become friendly with one praying man. I will use his initials for the reason being that I do not have his permission to use his name. IN, he was the principal of a local junior high school in Liberia.

IN was not only the principal of his school, he was also an intercessor that interceded for his school and some of his students when they were playing a soccer match or taking a public exam. I told him of how I have failed the WAEC twice and that I needed help.

He asked me by what means did I need his help; my answer to him was spiritually. "OK!" he said. "See me a month before you retake the exam."

When the exam time was approaching I, went to see him. He give me some psalms to read and a prayer to pray every day until the day of the exam.

The day before the exam, I went to see him. He prayed with me for about one hour. After which, I went home and slept. The next morning, I gave seven persons ten cents each and then took off to take the exam. The resetting that year was administered at the G. W. Gibson Junior High School, located on the capitol by pass.

## The Exam

Apart from fasting and praying, I was also studying. I'm really not a math person. It is just not my thing. As I sat down to take the exam, there were some of the problems there that I knew the answer and some of which I did not know the answer. The ones that I knew, I did; the ones I did not know, I guessed the answer since they were all multiple choice.

When the time allotted for the exam was over, the examiner—a lady—said, "Pencils down." As I laid my pencil down, something happened to me that I had never experienced before. My right eye winked three times, even though IN did not tell me that my eyes were going to wink. He only said, "As you take this exam, believe that you have passed, no matter what."

So when my eyes winked three times, I took it as a sign that all was well. Indeed when the result came out, I passed. I took this as a spiritual experience, which was the first of its kind. I was partly with my aunt back then.

Right after I had the experience with my right eye winking three times after the exam, it was not long that I had yet another experience while managing my aunt's shop. This time around, it was more profound.

The year before I was due to graduate from high school in December of 1984, my aunt opened a prevision shop in our home town of Pleemu, Todee District, Liberia. I conducted business at the shop as the manager. When it was time for me to go back to school, she employed a man to run the affairs of the shop. Which he did until sometime in 1986 when I retook over the management of the shop.

It was on a Thursday morning. Why I remember the day because it is like a national holiday in the chiefdom. Every Thursday is set aside as market day in Pleemu town; the day that people come from all over the district and counties to trade and also to buy goods.

# VOICE FROM MY HEART

On this day, I opened the shop as usual. After cleaning up the shop, I sat down, ready for business. The first money I made that morning was $0.75. I had three boys who live with my grandfather at the shop doing some work for me. Johnson Flomo, Robert Boo, and Junior Dibowou. They sat in front of the counter while I was behind the counter. I had my head bent down looking for something behind the counter.

With my head still bent down, I heard the voice speak to me from my heart, saying, "Anything the man asked you for, give it to him." The voice repeated itself three times in a split second.

Upon hearing the voice, I gently raise my head, only to see a man entering the shop. My eyes were fixed on him as he walked in. Without greeting anyone, he said to me, "Give me $0.75. I want to pay my way to go this way." Having being warned earlier by the voice, I gave him the $0.75, which was the first and only money I had made that morning since I opened the shop.

But instead of leaving, he sat down and asked me for my name. "What is your name?" "Emmett Shasha," I answered. He then said to me, "Give me a pen and a paper." Upon giving them to him, he again asked for my name. "Emmett Shasha," I answered. The man then said to me, "Let me help you." I said no at this point.

By then he had written something on the paper that I gave him that looked like Arabic. He again said to me, "Let me help you." Again, I said no to him. He said to me, "This is your hometown, and you love your people, but your people do not love you. I want to help, but you are saying no. Remember, I have told you that you love your people, but your people do not love you." With those words, he put down the paper and the pen that I gave him and left the shop. But whether he went up or down, that I don't know; only that I saw him walk out of the shop, that's all.

When he said to me, "Let me help you," I did not ask him what he meant. I only said to him no. The reason being that if he had come to help me as he was requesting, I would not have been warned concerning him by the voice, that I should give him anything that he asked me for.

What happened to me that night after my encounter with the strange man was terrible. Normally I will close the shop around 10:30-11:00 PM. All depending on the flood of customers. But at about 8:00-8:30 that night, my head began to hurt.

18

Within a short period, I began to experience water running down my nose, not mucus. My head hurt me so much that I closed the shop and went to bed.

I tried to fall asleep but was unable; I took some medication to help stop the headache, but it was to no avail. As I lay in bed, I really didn't know what time it was, but I heard a knock on the door.

"Emmett, Emmett," the person shouted my name while knocking on the door. I came to the door to see what it was that the person wanted; it was Bindna, my small aunt's husband, not my aunt who owns the shop.

"The pastor sent me to call you," he said. "We are having church service, and the Lord spoke to the pastor that he should send for you at once. To be prayed for, because where you are, your condition is not good."

Only God could have known that my head was hurting. Because when I closed down for the night, I told no one why. I locked the door and went with him. Like I said, I really didn't know what time it was. Just as we reached the church building, the lady on whom the spirit of prophecy was in operation. Her name is Kubono. She was well known in the church when it came to prophecy.

As we reached the church, upon entering the building, she began to speak out, "Pray for Emmett, pray for Emmett, the church should also take a three days' fasting and prayer for him says the Lord."

I stayed there that night until the service was over. By then they had prayed for me; the pastor also anointed me with oil.

I went home when the service was over. I came back to the church building to join in the fasting for the three days. While I was at the church, the shop was closed for business. Not being a committed Christian at the time, at the end of the three days of prayer and fasting I went to kakata to a man who was introduced to me by a family member.

It was believed that he communicated with familiar spirits. He told me that "the only reason why you are still alive today is because of your star." He then went on to tell me some things. "A man was sent to kill you," he said. "But the reason why he did not succeed is because of what you did for him." The man, whom I will name as Mr. Z, proceeded to describe to me the incident and how it all unfolded.

"It was on a day like market day," he said. "The place was packed with a lot of people. A man came to you in the shop where you are trading. He asked you for something, which you gave him. The thing that you gave the man was your way out because the person that sent him to kill you told him that you were very mean with the goods, and that you did not give anything to anyone who would asked. The concoction that was made with your name was done in a way that if the man that came to you to asked you for something, if you tells him no immediately upon his departure from you present you were to get sick and died."

If you remember, I mentioned earlier that a man came to the shop. The day it happened was on a Thursday. I also mentioned how he had asked me for $0.75 to pay his way to go someplace. What he said and what happened after he left was what brought me to see Mr. Z. All of what Mr. Z said were true to the best of my knowledge.

# THE TIME I MET
# JESUS CHRIST SPIRITUALLY

A few years later, some relative of mine passed away. I was told that before they passed, they confess to the elders of the town of what they intended to do unto me, how they had paid someone a (medicine man) to kill me.

I left Pleemu town in Pleemu clan of Todee District, from managing my aunt's provision shop, and moved back to Monrovia to attend school.

I enrolled at the Monrovia Vocational Training Center in Paynesvill Jacob's Town, Liberia, in 1987. While attending the MVTC, I again hooked up with Mr. IN, the principal of the local elementary and junior high school. I helped him fast for people when there was a need.

One time we fasted for about sixty days; it was the first time that I saw the Lord Jesus Christ in a dream after wherein I also saw angels ascending and descending from above. When I saw the Lord, it appeared in the dream that the whole world, the earth, was a savanna grassland, the earth was on fire but burning very slow. I began running to the center of the earth. There the Lord was standing. I ran until I reached him. He did not open his mouth to speak with me. He only spoke to me mentally, which I comprehend in my spirit. This is what he said: "What took you so long?" I did not reply. I only smiled as I drew closer to him.

After my training in woodwork at MVTC, I was sent out for my internship. I worked for LIPCO a furniture company on the bushrod Island. I also worked with the company that was constructing the national bank building opposite the E. J. Roy Building, located on Ashman Street in Monrovia.

My longtime friend and brother Stephen George, who worked as a teaching assistant at the University of Liberia back then and also as an instructor at the William V. S. Tubman high school in Sinkor Monrovia, came by to the place where I lived to discuss some things with me.

Before this visit, we had earlier met at the University Fendell Campus. He took me on a tour of the science complex, and we sat in the cafeteria; he ordered me food to eat while we talked. Before this talk, I had not seen Stephen for over five years, the reason being that just as he left the estate to live with his aunt, I also moved to Robertsport to attend school.

This meeting for us after five years was like a reunion. We talked of anything and about everything. After which, we started to visit each other. It was then that one day he came by at my place to have a discussion with me. At the time I lived in Jacob Town Paynesvelle, Liberia. He came to ask for my advice on what to do with the money he was about to receive from the government. He had not taken pay on his jobs for three months each, and now he was about to receive his paycheck for six months from both jobs.

I advised him to start a business. "Maybe a provision shop," I said. "Who will run the business?" he asked. "I can do it," I replied. We talked and talked, and then he left to go home. Stephen, I said earlier that he is a friend and brother. While I was in the eighth grade, he helped me with my assignment, especially math and physics.

When we met after the five years, our friendship grew to the point that we took an oath that in life, if anything was to happen to one of us, as in the case of death, the other person should take care of the other person's family.

He took my advice, and when he got his pay, I quit my internship job to start the shop. Just then the civil war in Liberia started. As the war intensified, so did the shop's growth—established by Stephen and managed by me. The shop was located on the old road opposite the Nigerian embassy. A school is now built where the shop once stood.

As the war drew closer and closer to Monrovia, I again began fasting and praying. Stephen came to the shop and told me that he had made arrangements for us to travel to Free Town, to escape the war. I deliberately delayed until the road to Free Town closed. It was cut off by rebel forces with allegiance to faction leader Prince Johnson.

Being so materialistic at the time, I didn't want to leave the goods in the shop. We had a huge consignment of goods in storage, and the shop itself was filled with goods.

It all changed on July 31, 1990, when government troops came and looted the shop. For me, that was the straw that broke the camel's back. I had to leave the government-held area to find safety in rebel-controlled territory. Which we later got to see that it was like leaving the frying pan and jumping into the fire.

The day was August 1, 1990; I have started fasting on the day before. We were nine who took off for rebel held territory. Just as we crossed the pavement leading to the German and Nigerian embassies, going by way of Congo town old road, the very same voice that had spoken to me from my heart years ago in 1986 again spoke to me.

The first time it took place I mentioned earlier was when I was managing my aunt's shop in Todee District Pleemu town. Back then the voice instructed me to give the man whatever he asked of me.

It was the same voice that once again spoke to me from my heart. "You are Joshua, you are Joshua, you are Joshua," just how the voice repeated itself thrice in 1986 to save my life. This time it was to give me courage. The reason being that when we left the house, fear paralyzed my heart, for the sound of guns was so intense that the smoke of gunpowder filled the air. I was really afraid. Just as the voice spoke to me, all fear departed from me. Even though the sound of guns still echoed in the air, it meant nothing to me.

I fasted all of July 31 up to August 1, 1990. When we left Sinkor old road, we slept at Mt. Barclay. The next day we went to the fendell Campus of the University of Liberia, that was now the home for over thirty thousand internally displaced Liberians. Unable to bear the sight of the people, starving from the lack of food, we made the decision not to stay but to move forward.

Since I was leading the group, I had to decide whether we will go to Crozerville or to Todee. Well, I chose to go to Todee, the reason being that under normal condition, my grandmother, brother, and cousins that lived in Crozerville all went to Todee to our grandfather when things and times were hard. Now that the country was upside down, it was only logical to go where we could survive.

As we journeyed from fendell campus, we reached the Voice of America junction (VOA for short). At that intersection stood an old Shell gas station that was now converted into a checkpoint by rebel commander. It took the grace of God for one to get across this checkpoint. We were on a line that was stretching over two miles long. So many, many people lost their lives at this checkpoint.

Some were suspected of being government officials running away, some were suspected of being soldiers that had dropped their uniform and were running away, others were people trying to get even with their enemies, etc. Upon reaching the checkpoint, the commander asked all that were there a question, "Do you see the flies? Do you smell the odor? It is not the smell of a dead animal, it is the smell of human beings. If you are not careful, you too will become like one of them."

It was frightening just to be present at this checkpoint. Like I said earlier about the day we left the government-controlled area for the rebel-controlled area, how the voice that had spoken to me from my heart some years ago spoke to me again that morning, and how that upon hearing the voice, all fear left me. Even as we stood at this checkpoint, I had no fear.

It's like what the scripture says in II Timothy 1:7: *"For God hath not given us the spirit of fear; but of power, and of love, and of a sound mind"* (Holy Bible, KJV). I was not afraid even though I had a reason to be afraid, but I just wasn't. As we were checked out, we crossed the checkpoint, passing the second house from the checkpoint.

A rebel soldier came to the door of the house after the checkpoint. He called out, "Ha, ha." As I turned to look, he called me. Upon reaching him, he asked me, "Where is the money you have?" I gave him a quarter that was in my right side pocket. Even though I had more money, I only gave him a quarter. He said, "Thanks, you can go." And we left.

# THE VOICE OF GOD

Leaving that house, we were now heading to the Careysburg township police station, which had also been transformed into a major checkpoint. By now we had been traveling for two days. About a thousand yards away from the checkpoint, I again heard a voice speaking to me. This time the voice did not come from my heart as the previous two did; it came from overhead. It sounded like it was going through the entire universe, yet I was the only one hearing it.

The voice like the ones that spoke to me from my heart was in plain English, crystal clear, and very soft spoken. As I listened to the voice, it was like it was echoing in the entire earth; yet of all the people that were walking with me, I was the only one that heard the voice.

I mentioned earlier of how the government troop had looted our provision shop. The day before the incident of the looting took place, I gave my brother Stephen George $3,000 from the sale of goods for safekeeping because the banks were closed. I took another $1,500 and put it under the freezer where we stocked the drinks that we sold. I did so because the freezer was very old with a hole in the middle of it that was also patched.

No matter what, I thought to myself, no one will remove this freezer. There was nothing on it to make it look attractive. Guess what? When I came back from behind rebel lines, the money was there waiting for me.

The very day we took off for rebel-held territory, I took $130 USD. I put it in a brown envelope and placed it in my right back pocket. The rest of the money from the shop I gave to Stephen. We left behind many goods.

We had traveled from Monrovia through Mt. Barclay, fendell campus, VOA checkpoint, and we were now headed to the Careysburg Police Station that was turned into another checkpoint. I heard the Lord speak to me (I say "the Lord" because right after I heard the voice, this scripture verse immediately came to mind: "Today, if ye will hear his voice, harden not your hearts, as in the provocation" [Hebrews 3:15 Holy Bible (KJV)]). At that moment, I did not know which book the scripture came from until I looked it up later. What I remember was "in these last days, when you hear the voice of the Lord, do not harden you hearts."

The sun was hot but not in its full strength. As the Lord spoke to me, this is what he said, "Give the money out, give the money out, give the money . . ." I reached my right hand into my right back pocket and took out the brown envelope containing the $130 USD. I gave the envelope to a young man who was traveling with us. Let's call him Mr. P.

He was from the Mano tribe, one of the tribal groups from where a large number of people came from to join the rebels. As he received the envelope, from my hands, he asked, "What is it?" I replied money. Without another question, he put the envelope in his pocket.

Upon reaching the checkpoint all of those whom I was traveling with went through the checkpoint. After they were checked, it was my turn. They took me inside a room to be checked. By then I weighed almost 225 lbs, my flesh overlapped my belt at my midsection. My breasts also overlapping a bit in my chest. This made me a perfect target for that of a former or a government official. My appearance showed that I was in the position of enjoyment.

In the room, they removed all of my clothes except for my underpants. As I stood there without clothing, they searched my entire pocket. They turned my bag inside out and found nothing. Then they asked me, "Where is your traveling allowance?" When I told them that I had no money, they then asked me, "What if we check you and find money with you. What should we do to you? At that, I say to them, "Anything."

A little boy, maybe three years older than my granddaughter who is now three, calling himself small soldier, reported that I was clear, meaning that I had no money. Based on the small soldier's report, I was ordered to put my clothes back on and get out. Because of the length of time that I had spent in the room, all of those whom I was traveling with were all now beginning to worry about my safety.

One thing I can say for sure is that when I heard the voice of the Lord telling me to give the money out, if I had not hearkened but rather hardened my heart against his warning, I would have died at that checkpoint for reasons mentioned earlier.

So many people in Liberia died during the war not because they bore arms. For some it was because of false accusation. Just as it is here in America, many people are in prison not because they committed the crime for which they are accused of but because of false allegations. My personal testimony for which this book is being written concerning false allegations, which is the highlight of this book, will be narrated soon.

In this portion, I will not use the name of the person I am about to mention because I do not have his permission. This man was a captain in the Armed Forces of Liberia. As the civil war heated up in Liberia, many people from the Gio and Mano tribes were disappearing overnight. At the end of the runway at the James Spriggs Field Air Field, in Sinkor, Monrovia was a killing zone, led by the death squad unit of the late President Samuel Doe. SATU, just as the ATU was to Charles Taylor. Who was the former rebel leader and former president.

See a bit of Doe's Special Anti-Terrorist Unit activities:

> **On December 24, 1989, a group of rebels operating under the umbrella of the National Patriotic Front of Liberia (NPFL), a warlordist militia under the leadership of Charles Taylor, entered Liberia through Cote d'Ivoire. The group consisted of an amalgam of individuals spanning Liberia's broad ethnic spectrum of sixteen indigenous groups, the settler, and other repatriate stocks. The group's primary objective was to remove the government of President Samuel Doe from power, and establish itself as Liberia's new rulers. Characteristically, the Doe regime responded to the threat with maximum force: It arrested, imprisoned, and murdered "suspected sympathizers" of the NPFL, and sent thousands of troops to the Liberian-Ivorian border to halt the incursion. For example, about 600 civilians, who took refuge in St. Peter's Lutheran Church in Monrovia, the capital city, were murdered by troops from Doe's dreaded Special Anti-Terrorist Unit (SATU).[2] This set into motion a bloody civil war that lasted for about eight years. The resultant effects included, among others, the deaths of thousands of innocent civilians, a refugee crisis, and the destruction of the country's already underdeveloped infrastructure.**
> (Religious leaders, Peacemaking, and the First Liberian Civil War [volume 2, Issue 2, Sparing 2009, first paragraph])

I will say a bit more about the St. Peter Lutheran Church murders later.

As I was saying, it was at the James Sprigge Airfield Runway that so many of the Gio and Mano people in Monrovia died. In case you are wondering how I got to know, Mr. P., the young man to whom I gave the money that was in the brown envelope to keep for me while we were approaching the checkpoint in Careysburg after the Lord had spoken to me, was a victim and a survivor who lived to tell the story only because he was also able to speak the Kpelle dialect, one of the local tribe, but he himself is from the Mano tribe. I will elaborate more about Mr. P. later.

A captain in the armed forces of Liberia, Mr. C., his wife and his daughter stopped by at the shop almost every day to buy goods. They knew me well, and I also knew them as well: a very good and loving family. Mr. C.'s house was located behind the Nigerian Embassy in Monrovia. Even though he was not from the Gio or Mano tribe, he used his rank as captain in the army to provide protection for those that were around his community, especially for the Gio and Mano tribes.

He provided protection for his neighbors. As the rebel closed in on the city, he told them that he would have to move his family to the center of town because the place where he lived was about to be run over by rebel forces. Few days after he left, the rebel forces overran the German, Nigerian, and many other foreign missions to Liberia that were located in that part of town. You can imagine Mr. C.'s home was of no exception.

# The Plight Of Mr. P

Mr. C. himself told me his story upon my return from the rebel territory, that one of the very boys whose parents he was protecting was the one who burned down his house. It was like what the scripture verse says in the book of Matthew 10:36, *"And a man's foes shall be they of his own household"* (Holy Bible, KJV). He was there for them when they needed him, but when the table changed, they could not do the same for him.

From this scenario, one can judge that if Captain C. had not left at the time that he did, both him and his family would have been dead. Why would he? Some may ask.

He was a captain in the army, for God's sake, and the army was deemed responsible for the disappearing of their tribal men Gio and Mano from where the young boy that burned down his house was from. One thing the young man that burned Mr. C. house forgot to know that if it were not for Mr. C., both he and his family would had also disappear overnight at the hands of the death squad. I mentioned the captain's story to let all who will read this book know why so many innocent people died in the war. Now concerning the young man Mr. P. who I gave the money to for safety, he was a friend of my brother Stephen. I got to know him from doing business with us at the shop. At the peak of our business before the war, we sold soft drinks and beer wholesale and retail. Mr. P., who was a medical student, lived partly on the medical compound of the JFK Memorial Hospital in Sinkor Monrovia. And at his house, he had a provision shop of his own that was managed by his wife when he was out at school. Our shop supplied his shop with soft drinks and beer. Apart from his provision shop, Mr. P. also had a financial club with the membership open to the public. Among his many members was an army officer. I will not state his rank nor will I give his name for security reasons on my part or that of my family and relatives still in Liberia.

He was the head of the death squad unit of SATU of the Armed Forces of Liberia. He lived on a road known as airfield shortcut. Mr. P. was well known by the head of the death squad unit and his immediate body guard also knew that he was from the Mano tribe.

As the war intensified, Mr. P. left his house to take up permanent residence in the JFK compound for fear for his life.

By moving to the compound, he thought that he would have been saved there. Boy oh boy! He was dead wrong; it was a mistake he will live to regret.

In the month of July 1990, few days before we left for the rebel-held area, Mr. P. said that very week that we were making preparations to go behind rebel lines that that's when his plight started. Of course he did not know that we were making plans to go behind rebel's lines. But considering the time, it was concomitant.

Mr. P. said while on the compound, a band of soldiers from the Armed Forces of Liberia went to the JFK medical compound and ordered every one out. They were told to come out with their hands over their heads. Being afraid that one of the soldiers might recognize him, he and some others went up in the attic of the building where they spent the night.

The next day, he and the others came down cautiously. By then the compound was empty. They made their way toward the gate into the street. Just as they exited the compound, they were all rounded up and ordered to board a military truck. They were taken to the end of the runway of the James Spriggs Field Airfield, in Sinkor Monrovia. Upon reaching there, they were all stripped naked. They were then made to form a straight line. One by one they were questioned, "What tribe are you?" If the person said Gio or Mano, that person was shot pointblank. If they were from another tribe, they were severely beaten and told to go. They made sure that the person spoke the dialect.

Before his eyes, Mr. P. saw some of those that were with him in the attic shot dead, others were severely flogged. Then came his turn, He was asked, "What tribe are you?" "Kpelle," he replied. "OK, speak Kpelle," they said. The little kpelle he knew he then began to speak it. He was hit with the gun bottom several times. They were beating him while saying to him, "You stupid kpelle man. Who told you to come here? We are looking for Gio and Mano people to kill. Who told you to come here? You stupid man."

Mind you, they were the ones who took him there in a military truck, now they were asking him, "Who told you to come here?"

After flogging him, they told him to go. When he asked them for his clothes, he was given two choices: go naked or receive his clothes and die. Upon hearing that, he left at once, going naked. He walked along the Tubman blvd. It was as if he was a mad man.

From the airfield runway, he walked until he reached the junction of the St. Joseph Catholic Hospital. He remembered having a doctor friend at the hospital, so he went in hoping that he will see the doctor friend. Perhaps he would be of some assistance to him.

As he reached the hospital, those that saw him ran away from him, thinking that he was a mad man. He was finally able to talk to a man, one of the hospital workers, who gave him a pair of pants and a shirt.

As he left the hospital, where to go was his thought. Going to his house was out of the question. His only thought was to go forward, not backward. It was in this moment that he remembered his friend Stephen, my brother. Our shop was about a mile up the road from where he was. He made his way to the shop.

Upon reaching the shop, he saw a girl and asked her where Stephen, the owner of the shop, is to which the girl replied, "I do not know Stephen only Emmett." "Where is this Emmett?" he asked. The girl then went to call me. I had the shop closed and was over at our neighbor's place who had given me a room in his house.

As I walked to the shop to see the person who was looking for me, I immediately recognized Mr. P. and called him by his name. He looked very frightened. Without thinking, I said to him, "Why is it that you are so frightened as though you were a gio man?" He smiled and said nothing. Until that day, I never knew that he was a Mano man. It was Stephen who told me that day as I later narrated the scenario to him.

He asked me for Stephen. When I told him that Stephen was out, he quickly asked me, "Is he coming back?" Yes, I said. He then took a deep breath of relief. He then said to me, "I have not taken a bath for I don't know how long, and I have not eaten for over three days."

I gave Mr. P. some warm water to take his bath and some toothpaste and a toothbrush. When he was done, I gave him two cans of Vinto and some food to eat. Later that evening, Stephen came, and Mr. P.'s spirit to live returned. By daybreak the next day, the first of August 1990, we all left to go behind rebels lines.

This is how I got to know Mr. P. Leaving the checkpoint in Careysburg, we walked until we got to fifteenth gate. It was here that Mr. P. then left our group to go to Firestone where he lived many years go. By now we were only four persons left in our original group of nine. Fortunately for us, no one died from the group. Passing fifteenth gate, we reach Number 7. Fifteenth gate, Number 7, these are the names of various town along the kakata Monrovia highway. At Number 7, there was another rebel gate. We were again told to form a single file, meaning that we should form a straight line. I must admit that in the third day of our journey, we were almost used to it because every gate we came across, we were told to form single file.

The line was very long. In the line, I was about two hundred to 250 feet away from the checkpoint. A man standing at the door of the building which services as the checkpoint office lifted up his hand and began to called out, "Ha, you come here." Not knowing who he was calling, almost everyone in the line were asking, "Me? Me? Me?" It was one "Me?" after another until it was my time.

I lifted up my right hand as the others before me did. "Me?" I asked. "Yes, you," the man replied. "Come here." Oh, boy! I thought. I was not happy at all because I did not know what to expect. But I was not afraid.

# THE PRAYERS OF ELISHA

By now, I knew that if my life was involved, I would have heard the Lord speak to me from above or from my heart, of what to do. Without any warning, I knew it was OK. But I just wasn't happy. I got out of the line and walked past all those that were in front of me. On reaching the checkpoint, immediately I recognized the man that was doing the calling, not as a friend but one who I blasted at in the past during normal days (when the country was at peace).

How I met this man it was before the war. I was traveling from Bong Mines (a mining town in lower Bong County) to Kakata. I purchased my ticket and got on the bus. The man at the checkpoint was in the driver's seat of the bus. When the bus was filled, the man drove off. All we knew was that he was the driver of the bus until the worst happened. Nearing Miss Moore Mission (a boarding school) on the Bong Mines, Kakata highway, this man ran the bus off the road over the dirt almost dumping the bus into the swamp. Thanks be to God that it did not happen, but the bus was going to turn over.

Just as the bus was running off the road to fall into the swamp, a police car was approaching and saw everything unfolding. Speaking of perfect timing, that was it. When the bus finally stopped, the driver quickly came to the back of the bus while the conductor quickly made his way to the front of the bus. When the police arrived, they asked for the driver. At that, the conductor presented himself as the driver and gave his license.

I immediately protested. "No! No! He is not the driver," I told the police. "The man that gave you his license was not the one driving the bus, he was the conductor on the bus." The police then asked a general question, "Who was driving this bus?" All the other passengers kept their mouths closed. No one said a word. I then told them all, "If this bus had capsized and there was to be any survivor, I would have been the only one." The police helped as we pushed the bus back on the road. Still in running condition, the police escorted the bus to Kakata. Once all the passengers were out of the bus, the real driver and his conductor were taken to the police station for questioning while I continued my journey to Monrovia.

It was the conductor now turned rebel that was standing at the door calling out. Even though I immediately recognized him, I noticed that he did not recognize me. Speaking of protection, I was being protected by God very much. While it is true that I did not pray this payer as the prophet Elisha did when he said, *"Smite this people, I pray thee, with blindness. And he smote them with blindness according to the word of Elisha"* (II Kings 6:18).

In reality, I prayed while also reciting the Ninety-first Psalms, believing the wordings of this psalm shielded me as the Bible says. I believe strongly that the Lord blinded the eyes of the man from recognizing me. Upon reaching the door, the man asked me, "Who are those that you are traveling with? Call them." I called all my traveling companions. Without anyone's bags being checked, we all walked through the checkpoint.

How good can the goodness of God get? The man then said to me, "I really like you. I don't want you to walk any farther. I will find a car to take you to Kakata." Upon saying those words, he left us and went back to his post at the checkpoint. Because he had said that I should not walk or that he didn't want me walking, we waited to see if he would find us a car. Of course the only cars running if you saw one was commandos operation cars/trucks. After a few minutes, he came back to me and pleaded with me that I should not walk, that the road ahead was very dangerous. *Could it be anything more than we have experienced?* I thought to myself.

As he was talking, we saw a man coming from the bush behind the checkpoint with a knife in his hands that had blood on it. The man then said to me, "Do you see that man with the knife in his hand?" I said yes. "He's coming from killing a girl," the man said. I asked him, "Why? What did she do?" He said that the girl was carrying an album in her hand that had the president's (Samuel Doe) picture in it. In that light, she was seen either as a family member of the president or a close friend of the president.

We rested while awaiting a car that never came. We spent the night in a house that was not far away from the checkpoint. At the first light of day, we took our things and continued our journey. As we left the house, I did not see the man, and I did not ask about him. As we took off, it was now four days since we left the government-held area of Monrovia for Pleemu, which was under rebel's control.

As I stated how the Lord must have blinded the man's eyes to prevent him from recognizing me, this was not the first time but the second of three such events. If the Lord had not done it, I would have died at this checkpoint.

If the man had recognized me as being the one who ran my mouth to the police back then, he would have said to me, "Do you remember me some years ago when you made the police to arrest me? Now is my turn." Thanks be to God for his intervention. Like I said, the blinding of the man's eyes by the Lord was not the first but the second of three occurrences. I mentioned earlier of how the government troops had gone to our provision shop and looted it. I was sitting in the shop with the door half open. The voice did not speak to me on the thirty-first of July, it was on the first of August 1990. But as I sat there, I got this strong sentiment that I should leave from where I was because something bad was about to happen. At once, I closed the shop and hurried and went outside to my friend's house that was on the other side of the fence near the shop. This friend who is now a pastor in Liberia joined me that day for a fast. In his house were a lot of displaced people. Among this group was a young man from the Gio tribe who was shot in the back. The gunshot did not go through his body but stuck in his flesh. The shot was removed by doctors at the St. Joseph Catholic Hospital.

The young man was shot while seeking refuge at the St. Peter Lutheran Church in Sinkor, Monrovia,

> On Sunday, July 29, 1990 about 3 a.m. in the morning more than 900 Liberians taking refuge in the St. Peter's Lutheran Church and parsonage were massacred. It was a few months into the civil war, and then leader Samuel Doe was fighting Charles Taylor, a former member of his regime. Charles Taylor's father was one of those refugees"

Posted by jenniferbeaumont on 1/11/12 • Categorized as
Adventure travel, Black history, Solo travel, Travel

My friend and I sat outside in the garage of his house, which had no gate; the place was wide open. The fence between his house and the shop was about four feet high.

While one group of soldiers looted the shop, two others came to the back of the shop. Leaning on the wall of the fence and using their arms for supporters, they began to talk. The fence wall was made of six-inch blocks. In their discussion, one said to the other, "What's about this house? Let's check it out." "No!" the other replied. "It is empty, can't you see it?" Meanwhile, my friend and I were sitting in the garage looking and listening to them as they talked. There was no way that they could not have seen us, because we were visibly exposed. We were looking at these men face-to-face. For them to not to see us, it must have been the Lord who had blinded their eyes from seeing us. Not only that, but he also kept them from entering the fence. The distance between us must have been only twenty to thirty feet. If those soldiers' eyes were not blinded by the Lord, if they had entered the fence and searched the house they would have seen the young man that was shot at the Lutheran church, since in fact the killing that took place at the church was committed by the government soldiers. Seeing this man among us, we would have all been labeled as rebel supporters or rebel sympathizers. Our penalty would have been death.

When the looting was over, their friends called out to them. They all got in their cars (a brown Mercedes Benz and a Mitsubishi jeep) and drove away. On another occasion, before the looting of the shop by the troops, a lady came to the shop to purchase some items. While she and I were talking, I got this strong sentiment that something bad was about to happen nearby. I then told the woman, "You must come into the shop now so that I can close the door." "Why," she asked. "I have to go home," I said to her. "You will go home later, but you have to wait a bit and come inside while waiting." She came in, and just as I closed the door, the sound of gunfire erupted about a hundred feet from the shop, multiple guns sounded. Within a few minutes, the shooting was over. I reopened the shop, and the lady went home. Two days after that incidenct, the same lady came back to buy some things. She asked me, "How did you know the other time that something was about to happen?" To which I replied, "I don't know, but before it did, I just knew it." "Very strange," she said. "Yep," I replied.

From Number 7, we walked until we reached Pleemu town in Pleemu clan in Todee District. This was on the fourth day since we left Monrovia. While in Pleemu, we made gardens and did other farm work.

After some time in Pleemu, Stephen and I took off for Bong mines. We were there until the money we had ran out. We then went on my aunt's farm to live. While there, we helped with all of the farm work. Later we decided to burn fire coals to earn us some money. By the time we were done with the coals burning, we got ninety-five bags of coals, after which, we went back to Pleemu.

Back in Pleemu, in the month of September 1990, my mother and stepmother were out on the farm. My father, the late Lewis J. Shasha, a.k.a. Bob Lewis, was at home. Just as it had happened in the past, I got the feeling that something bad was about to happen, but not in my immediate surroundings. I told my father that something bad was about to happen. He asked me, "Like what?" I said I don't know but it will be very bad. I was still speaking to my father when we heard the sound of a gun.

Few minutes later, a group of rebel commandos came to our house. They killed our dog and took it with them. We then learned that the sound of gun that we heard earlier was on a young man, one of our friends. He was shot in the leg by the rebel for no apparent reason. My father again asked me, "How did you know that something bad was about to happen?" "I don't know," I replied. "But I just knew it."

# The Sentiments That Warns me of Dangers & Conspiracy Against my Father

In the month of December 1990, on Christmas Day to be exact, we had gathered some cassava that day to be used to bake ourselves some cassava bread. My father had gone to my grandfather's house while my little sisters and cousin got the cassava ready for us to bake the bread. I was the one to supervise the baking because I knew about the cassava bread. While waiting for them, we were all happy playing and rejoicing, making a lot of noise because after all, it was Christmas Day.

Just then I got this very strong sentiment that something very, very bad was about to happen, and it was going to take place in my immediate circle even in our house. I called my stepmother and told her that we needed to pray. Other than that, we were not going to spend the day well. I prayed and tried to beat the feeling off. The more I tried, the more it intensified. I left and went into the room by myself to see if the Lord will show me what was about to happen. I tried to close my eyes, but it was hard. All I was sensing was danger, danger all around me. I was not really afraid, but I did not know what to do.

I got up from the bed and came back outside. I managed to bake the bread, but I could not get my mind from wondering what it was that was going to take place.

I spoke of going in the room by myself to see if the Lord was going to show me something. The first time I did such a thing was in December of 1983, while attending the St. John Episcopal High School in Robert Sport Grand Capemount County Liberia. I was in the tenth grade, hoping for a promotion to the eleventh grade. We were done with all of our final exams. It was only a week for school to close.

It was right after lunch that day, I got the strong sentiment that something just wasn't right. You could say it was my first spiritual experience, only that I did not recognize it as such. At once, I decided to find out just what it was that wasn't going right. I left everyone outside and walked to my dorm room. Once there, I lay on my bed and placed a small pocket-sized New Testament on my chest. Very deeply engulfed with this sentiment, I closed my eyes. As I did intensely, I found myself standing in the principal's office. At that particular moment in real life, all the faculty members were meeting in the principal's office. As I entered the office in the spirit realm, I heard the principal ask, "What about Emmett Shasha? He has 69 average in social studies." The teachers said, "He is a nice boy and very respectful." The principal then said, "OK, we will add 10 points to the 69 to equal the 79 average, which will enable him to pass." They all agreed. At that, I was back in my body but did not leave the room because the feeling was still strong upon me.

As I laid there in bed, the whole episode was repeated three times, after which I got up, knowing that all was well. What I saw in the spiritual realm was very real. Indeed after the final exam, my average in social studies was 69 percent. When I received my report card, the first place I looked was at my social studies, and sure enough, I had for my final average 79, a passing grade. The 69 percent would have sent me to summer school.

We ate the cassava bread and enjoyed the moonlight that Christmas night, I almost forgot about the feel I had on Christmas Day until the early afternoon of the twenty-sixth of December 1990, when rebel commandos filled our town. They arrested every able-bodied men that were in the town. They were all made to sit on the road in the middle of the town. With all the men that were in Pleemu town now rounded up and made to sit on the road, the commanders split into two groups. One group headed to my grandfather's town (Japan's Town) while the other was left behind to oversee the men from Pleemu Town.

Upon reaching Japan's town, they again rounded up all the men that were in town and made them to sit in the middle of the road. My father was among the men sitting on the road. I told the commanders that I had to reach my grandfather who was old and partly blind. They allowed me to leave the group sitting on the road to go to my grandfather.

On reaching my grandfather, when he saw me he said, "Sonny, Sonny, what's wrong? What is going on?" I responded, "I don't know, Dad, but they want you to come out of the house." While Emmett is my name, my grandfather had a nickname for all of his grandchildren. I guess mine was Sonny. Sometimes he called one person Captain or "How you doing, Honorable?" So for me it was always Sonny. That's how he called his grandchildren most of the time when he was still alive. The rebel ransacked my grandfather's house, taking valuables and whatever they could lay their hands on.

They then took all of the men from my grandfather town and brought them to Pleemu town. By now fear had left me because I was doing more praying in my heart than talking.

My grandfather was given a place to sleep for the night in Pleemu town. He slept in the house of a friend of our family. My father, one of the young men that lived with my grandfather, and I were placed in a room along with some other men from the town of Pleemu. The rebel commander nailed the windows and put an armed man on guard at the door during the night.

During the night, my father wanted to drink water. He asked a lady that lived in the house where we were being kept for some water. The lady told my father, "Sorry, I don't want to be a part of what is happening." She did not give him the water. Mind you, this was the woman that came to our house every day, asking my parents for things. On the other hand, as I look back, the woman was afraid. What she said, I believe, was out of fear. The room in which we were placed had a small mat about three feet wide and about four feet long. I took it and sat on it; it was that mat that was used as a bed that night by my father. The young man who lived with my grandfather and I to sleep on. I was so ashamed and embarrassed, the reason being that my father was sleeping on the floor, lying beside me, and there was nothing that I could do about it.

That night, I did not talk. I really did not sleep. What I did was that I prayed from my heart all night. By daylight, I knew that all was well. The feeling of peace came over me. The young man who was with my father and me who slept (or should I say was lying on the floor with us) was Robert Boo. He was one of the boys that was working for me in the shop when I was managing my aunt's business four years ago when I first heard the voice speaking to me from my heart, back in 1986. That I should give the man whatever he asked for.

That morning, the rebel commander took my father and some of the men from Pleemu town to Kakata, to the G-2 office. This G-2 office was the police station doing normal days, when there was peace. This was the same police station turned G-2 office where the rebel commander at the checkpoint in Number 7, the one who said that he did not want me walking; was taken for questioning when he almost ran the bus into the water as we traveled from Bong mines to kakata. As I mention earlier.

My little brother Vannie, now a pastor, and I along with two persons from my grandfather's town followed my father to kakata. On December 26, 1990, when rebel commander came to Pleemu town and Japan towns and rounded up all the men, the accusation against us was that we were aiding rebel faction leader Prince Y. Johnson of the INPFL, Independent National Patriotic Front of Liberia. This accusation was not only false but baseless and was being used as a means of exploiting people they thought had some money or anything they wanted.

While still in Monrovia in the government-held area, I learned from the BBC that Charles Taylor's (the Liberian rebel leader) number two man, Prince Johnson, had broken away from the NPFL (National Patriotic Front of Liberia) to form the INPFL. The BBC referred to Prince Johnson as being very swift and unstoppable. Upon reaching my home town of Pleemu from Monrovia, I learned from my father and others that while on his way to capture the Todee Military Base, Prince Johnson and his men passed through our town. His men put my grandfather out of his house, which was then prepared for their leader. He slept in the house of my grandfather for two nights and also forced some of the boys from Japan's town to carry his load when he took off.

Prince Johnson passed through the town of Pleemu long before I arrived there on August 4, 1990. Remember I mentioned that we left Monrovia August 1, 1990. We traveled for four days before reaching Pleemu on August 4, 1990. By the time we reached Pleemu, Prince Johnson was already on the outskirts of the capital Monrovia. It was Prince Johnson and his men who captured the road leading from Monrovia to Freetown Sierra Leone, thus preventing Stephen and I from traveling to Freetown. So for Charles Taylor's men to come months after Prince Johnson had passed through our town and say that we were supporting him is mind-boggling.

Like I said, my brother and I along with some others went to kakata to bring my father back home. Upon reaching kakata, we were informed that my father was put in prison at the G-2 office. I have never lived in kakata before; only my mother did before the war, so I really didn't know where to start with regard to contact. Besides, this was wartime, not normal days. We were now living under the control of rebel's commander.

My brother and I began walking in the streets of kakata city. We passed by way of the marketplace, which was located near the Lanko Lapy Junior high school. There we met a young man, and he was very intelligent but looked a bit drunk. By divine intervention, we started a conversation. I got to know that he was a former student from the Cuttington University College. I told him that one of my cousins was also at the university. When I mentioned my cousin's name, the man said, "Oh, that's my brother," referring to my cousin. We talked a bit, and then I told him of my father. He asked me, "Where is your father now?" I said, "At the G-2 office, in prison."

The man then asked us to walk with him to the G-2 office. My brother and I walked with the man. By then it was getting dark. We reachrd the G-2 office. I was shocked when we reached the G-2 office. All of the commander that were there of various rank stood at attention to greet the man as we entered the building; they all saluted him.

Wow! I thought to myself, *This is no ordinary man.* The man asked for my father. They told him that he was locked up behind bars. He ordered my father out. The man then said to my father, "Old man, I could let you go home tonight, but we are many, and I don't want anyone to do you harm. I could let you go home tonight, but someone could harm you for nothing, so I want you to spend the night here. I will send you home tomorrow morning. Do not see yourself as being in prison. Just consider it as one of those things that a man have to experience in life." Those were the man's comforting words to my father; he then instructed the commander that my father should stay out as long as he wants and should only be put back in the cell upon his request.

The man then said to me, "Meet me here at 7:00 a.m." I said yes and left to find a place to sleep. The next morning, I did not show up at the G-2 office until 8:00 am.

I thought to myself that the man might come late because he appeared to be a bit drunk to me. Upon reaching the G-2 office the next day, December 28, 1990, at 8:00 am, I saw the man standing on the steps. "I told you to be here at 7:00 a.m." "Yes, sir," I replied with a smile on my face. The man then said to me, "Go to where your mother once lived before the war. There you will see your father." I said thanks to him, and without asking for his name, I took off running. I found my father sitting at the house where my mother once lived. There he was safe and sound. Later that day, my little brother and I took our father home back to Pleemu town. It was a happy reunion when we got back home. The night that my father was in the cell at the G-2 office, he got to know that his arrest should not had taken place on the twenty-sixth, rather it should have been on the twenty-fifth of December because the order for his arrest was given on the twenty-fifth at 8:00 a.m. What happened was that a boy from our town who became a member of the NPFL of Mr. Charles Taylor was at the G-2 office on Christmas morning. He now was a commando (the boy from our town that is) along with others and were discussing on where to go and who they could harass in other to get some money. It was at that time that the boy from our town told his fellow commandos, "You know, Prince Johnson is now in Monrovia, but on his way there he passed through our town, spending two nights in old man Shasha's house, the town next to our town. All you guys have to do is grab his son Lewis who lives in our town. That will cause him to release (give some money)."

According to the information, one of the commanders asked, "What crime will we charge him with?" Another said, "Ha, you are here, but your ear is not here (meaning that he was not paying attention). Did you not hear that Prince Johnson slept in the man's father's house? All we have to say is that we got information that the man is supporting Prince Johnson."

With that discussion, the plot to invade Pleemu and Japan towns was made. But the boy who brought out the idea was not going to be a part of the raid because he was known in the town. Mind you, while this discussion was taking place nine miles from Pleemu, it was at the exact same time when I got the overwhelming sentiment that something bad was about to happen in our home, and then I told my stepmother that we had to pray or else we were not going to spend (Christmas) the day right.

I spent few more months in Pleemu after the West African Peacekeeping troops arrived in Monrovia.

New Year's Eve, we had to travel to another town for the watch night service. We had lots and lots of fun. At the church, we had an outdoor program followed by the watch night service itself.

We were singing from Katota where we had the watch night service until we reached Pleemu. We ended up in Japan's town there I met my father. We hugged a long time, and I cried and cried. My father placed his hands on my back and said, "It's OK, Emmett, it's OK."

Not too long after that we then left Pleemu for Monrovia, again walking going back to Monrovia, just how we had walked at first leaving from Monrovia.

# THE TASTE OF FREEDOM

We passed this time by way of Crozerville. It was much closer to the buffer zone set up by the peacekeeping troop between the INPFL and the NPFL rebel faction. As we made it across the rebel's lines into the arms of the peacekeepers, we were warmly received and given some food. Man! It felt so good getting the taste of freedom again even though the war was far from over. But at that moment, it sure did feel like a heavy weight had been lifted off my shoulder. It felt like normal days again.

The buffer zone was in White Plains. We had to cross the St. Paul River to continue our journey to Monrovia under the guardianship of the peacekeepers. The other way would have been to to go from White Plains through Caldwell to Monrovia, but taking this way would mean that we were going to reenter another rebel zone of the INPFL. We did not want to do that.

After we crossed the St Paul River by a boat provided by the peacekeepers, we then had to pay our own way to board a pickup truck to take us to Monrovia. Everything looked different. I mean, they were just different. Life looked very normal under the peacekeepers. I saw the handprint of war everywhere. I was sad for the condition of the country but happy that I was out of the rebel-controlled area. As we boarded the pickup truck heading to Monrovia, I heard for the first time a music by the South African musician Lucky Dube. In one of his music, he spoke of wars as not being good.

He said people who knew nothing about the war and the government, women and children along with lots and lots of innocent people, were killed. To this I say he's very right. I mention of the many times I should have died had God not intervened.

By the time we returned to Monrovia, we found out that we had lost everything that we left behind when we went behind the rebel's line.

The shop where we once conducted our business was still there but empty. Amazingly, the old freezer was still in the shop. I decided to look under it to see if the $1500 money I had put there for safekeeping was still there. Sure enough, to my amazement, it was there. It was that money that we used to start selling kerosene. Stephen George, a professor at the University of Liberia, my brother, and I sold kerosene. Later we credited some money from a friend to reopen the shop.

It was not long after that my longtime girlfriend, who is now my wife, and I moved in together. I was first baptized at the age of nine. On my birthday, June 10, 1970, in Christ Episcopal Church, Crozerville, Montserrado. I did not know Christ for myself until four years later. I was attending the Assembly of God Mission School. By then, apart from the general prayer at school and the Lord's Prayer along with the Twenty-third Psalm taught to me by my grandmother (Ruth), I did not know how to pray.

It happened that on this particular day I got home from school. After doing my work, I sat on the front porch and began to sing. As I did, it was like someone asked me a question, "Who are you that a king should die for you?" At that age, I was not involved in any major sin, but yet I felt sorry for my sin. I then went into the room to pray, but I didn't know how to pray. All I said was "Lord, please forgive." Upon saying those words, I felt the presence of someone standing in the room. They had on a long white robe. From my intuition, they placed their right hand on my head. I felt anew. I was fourteen years old by then.

Later on when I got married, I was rebaptized in 1995. Before then I had rededicated my life to our Lord Jesus. By this time, I knew him for myself. While coming up as a young man, I made a vow to God. Even though I did not have a personal relationship with him, I knew enough to make a vow. Naive you can say, but I made the vow that the first woman that was going to give birth to a child for me would be the woman I was going to marry. Talk about reversing a straight path; that's what I did. It should have been marriage first before baby, but I had baby before marriage. Sure enough, Laverne gave birth to our first child who lived for twenty-one days and then passed away. In honor of my vow to God, I married my longtime girlfriend. Our wedding was a traditional one; as such the full customary laws of the land were applied. Today we have a houseful.

After our wedding, things and time were really hard; jobs were not forthcoming, companies and government were not paying their employees—things were just hard. By now Stephen and I were forced to relocate the shop. In so doing, we used the funds we had to purchase a piece of land and build a new shop, which left us without money to continue the business. Because of that, I had to get a job and relocate, leaving the building with Stephen to live in.

I got a job with JD Machine Works. Because the job was not paying enough, I made gardens to help bring in additional income. We planted eggplants, peppers, bitter balls, and caller grains to help take care of me and my family. It was the caller grains that brought in the most money. Our children sold the harvest every other Saturday, which brought in an income of about a thousand five to a thousand six hundred Liberian dollar every two weeks. We used the money we got from our produce along with my pay from work to take care of our family.

By now, the voice had not spoken to me for years. One day I got home from work. I went about thirty minutes' walk from our house to get some herbs. Just as I entered the bush and commence picking the herbs, the sentiments of imminent danger came over me, I knew that I had to leave at once, not walking but running. I do not know what danger it was, but I knew that whatever it was, it had to be very serious and dangerous in order for me to receive that emergency alert.

A month after this incident, I was coming home from work. Along the road I heard about something concerning one of my daughters. That made me so mad. I decided that when I got home, I was going to beat her for it. But before reaching our house, I had to pass by the Catholic Church. Upon reaching the church building, the voice that had first spoken to me from my heart in 1986 and 1990 again spoke to me from my heart in 1997. "Don't beat Lorpu. Don't beat Lorpu. Don't beat Lorpu." Three times it repeated itself just as it did in the past.

When I got home that night, my family had just come from having their evening devotion, something we did every morning and every evening. After greeting them, I then said to my daughter, "You must have been praying because as I was on my way home thinking of beating you, the Lord spoke to me on the road not to beat you." From that day on, I never again laid hands on any of my children to beat them.

I had to travel to Tubmanburg, Bomi, to work. When we got there we were lodging at the St. Dominic School campus, of course there was no school in session at that time. People were displaced, dead, or missing. The country was divided with almost every sector of Liberia being ruled or under the control of some warring factions.

We cleaned up the school building and made it ready to be used as a feeding center. We also built other centers. As the people began returning from the bushes where they were hiding, it became obvious that more and more rooms were needed to accommodate the people. We were asked to relocate off the school campus.

While in the process of finding a place in the city, we met the acting superintendent appointed by the warlord of ULMO-J of Roosevelt Johnson whose territory we were working in. He took us to his house and gave us two rooms. My supervisor said that we should take our things and move in that same day. I told him to wait; he asked me why. I told him to give me at least three days. I did not tell him why the three days, but I was expecting the Lord to speak to me concerning our moving.

That night, I found myself in a night vision. In the vision it appeared as though I had gone to buy some goods from a local shop. While there, I saw the acting superintendent I asked him in the vision, "The place you gave us, is it still available?" To which he said yes and invited me to go with him to see the place. Just as I was about to walk with him, a brown dog came from nowhere. It began to bark at us, trying to prevent us from moving.

I took a piece of stick and began to shoo the dog. I was looking at the dog when it ran off, for some reason unknown to me. I kept on looking at the dog. All of a sudden, the dog changed into a very beautiful little girl. She was wearing a pink nightgown. She did not open her mouth to talk, but looking at her, I heard her speaking to me without making a sound.

With the same impression, I heard her speak; I also replied her without opening my mouth. As I looked at her, what I understood was that she was saying to me "Do not go with him." I then asked her, "You don't want me to go with him?" At that, she nodded her head to indicate no. I then understood that I was not to move into the place that was provided by the acting superintendent.

In the morning, I told my supervisor that we were not moving into the place that had been provided to us. "Why?" he asked. "Trust me on this one," I told him. "We are not moving in. You can if you want to, but I will not." That was the end of that conversation.

We move into a house owned by a lady who was a pastor. I mentioned this because many of such visions in different form had played out in my life since I arrived in this country. Let it be known that I (Emmett) stand by every word and bit of information contained in this book.

I had the opportunity of attending a seminar on entrepreneurship, which was organized by an international NGO, GTZ (German Technical Corporation). It was sponsored by the UNHCR. Upon the completion of the seminar, those that passed receive a certificate of completion. After which, we were each treated as entrepreneurs and given projects to implement. The various projects were known as QIP-Standard Profile.

I had to travel from Monrovia to Nimba County, the northern part of Liberia. It was at the end of the disarmament period. As a means of reintegrating former combatants into mainstream society as part of the project agreement, every project manager/supervisor had to employ some former combatants.

During the project, I got to know that some of the former combatants we employed were not former combatants at all. Rather they were active member of Charles Taylor Anti-Terrorist Unit (ATU), which was one of the most notorious armed groups in Liberia. Because I did not give in to their demands, to let them have their ways with the materials, we were not on good terms.

I filed numbers of complains with the field officer of GTZ, which had direct supervision over these projects, but it was to no avail. The reason being that these field officers were themselves afraid of these so-called former combatants. The project was delayed for a month because of the problem I was encountering with those so-called ex-combatants.

God first. My life should have ended on this earth physically while in Nimba County. I got so many death threats. Thanks be to God for using the general town chief and paramount chief who provided security that lasted until the completion of the project.

When these former combatants/ATU personnel saw that they could not get rid of me in Nimba County, they had a meeting discussing that they should lie low until we went back to Monrovia, and that at the first glance of any trouble in the city, I was going to be treated as an enemy of the government. Upon hearing this, my thoughts were to leave the country before anything of such nature occurred. This of course came to pass right after I left the country for the States. Here is an article from human right watch:

> The ATU had no legal basis for its existence, and was not under the command of the Ministry of Defense. The ATU absorbed Taylor's most experienced NPFL civil war fighters, including undisciplined and untrained loyalists. There were many unlawful killings by security forces during 2002. For example, on June 19, an ATU officer and presidential guards opened fire on a taxicab in Monrovia and killed a 6-year-old child and critically injured his mother and the driver. President Taylor ordered an investigation of the incident, which was ongoing at year's end.
> Human Rights Watch

# LIVES COMPARISONS & FORMAL INTRODUCTION

Our establishments work on QIP Number 92, which was the Construction and Renovation of the Larpea NO. 1 Public School. Nimba/ Gbehlay—Geh/Larpea No.1. As the field supervisor, I had ninety working days to complete the project. The budget for the project was USD $36,931.75. Thanks be to God that at the completion of the project, both the GTZ and the UNHCR graded the project the best of the five projects, which were implemented in Nimba County that year.

When I commence the writing of this book, I said in the beginning that the plight that came upon Joseph in Egypt, as recorded in the book of Genesis chapter 39, is the motivating factor that has driven me to sit down and compose this material. As we look back at Joseph's story today, we can all acknowledge that in the story he was an innocent man who was falsely accused of a crime he knew nothing about.

For safety's sake, along with the desire to live in America, I left Liberia and traveled to the United States of America. I spent about a month and a half in Boston. After I arrived in this country on March 11, 2001. I then moved to Columbus Ohio where I still live today. Once in Columbus, I began the processing of my paperwork for legitimacy. It was all completed in 2011 when I took the oath and became a citizen of the United States. While it is true that I am not as old as Jacob, father of Joseph, when his son Joseph presented him to the Pharaoh, yet the answer given to Pharaoh by Jacob when he inquired his age I sometime feel exactly the same way he felt. *"And Joseph brought in Jacob his father, and set him before Pharaoh: and Jacob blessed Pharaoh. And Pharaoh said unto Jacob, How old art thou? And Jacob said unto Pharaoh, The days of the years of my pilgrimage are an hundred and thirty years: few and evil have the days of the years of my life been, and have not attained unto the days of the years of the life of my fathers in the days of their pilgrimage"* (Gen.47:7-9)

I identified with this statement *"few and evil have the days of the years of my life been"* because nowhere in my wildest dream could I have ever imagined that the nation that is highly respected for human rights avocation will be the very nation subjecting it's residents and citizens to mental torture. When one makes up lies about another and spread false rumors about them, dehumanizing and demonizing, them please tell me as you read on in the end if it is not a violation of their basic human rights. Please tell if this will not affect you emotionally and physically.

My life in America, Columbus Ohio that is, I compare it to that of Joseph's life after he was bought from the slave market and taken to the house of Prospered. It all started at 4336 Thornapple Circle West, Columbus Ohio 43231. If there was ever a time that the spiritual part of me was active, the time is now.

I mentioned Joseph, son of Jacob, how that my life in America is compared to that of his life in the house of Potiphar in Egypt. At that time, I did not go into details. But before going any further, I would like to throw a little light on some Bible characters that was faced with almost what I am going through. By doing so, I believe it will help you understand the book better and enable you to see the reality of my plight. Was it destined to be? Was it a part of God's plan for my life? A bad karma or just one of life's many circumstances? I don't know, but if Joseph's story was not recorded in the Holy Bible for all to read, upon hearing his story by word of mouth, as humans, the first conclusion would be he is guilty as accused. The statement by Potiphar wife as recorded in these verse was what sent Joseph to prison. But in reality, who knew the truth? And how many persons believed the lies that was told by his master's wife? *"And it came to pass about this time, that Joseph went into the house to do his business; and there was none of the men of the house there within. And she caught him by his garment, saying Lie with me: and he left his garment in her hand, and fled, and got him out. And it came to pass, when she saw that he had left his garment in her hand, and was fled forth, That she called unto the men of her house, and spake unto the men of her house, and spake unto them, saying, see he hath brought in an Hebrew unto us to mock us; he came in unto me to lie with me, and I cried with a loud voice: And it came to pass, when he heard that I lifted up my voice and cried, that he left his garment with me, and fled, and got him out"* (Gen. 39:11-15)

The truth was known only by three persons, Joseph master's Potiphar wife, Joseph himself, and the third person of the trinity, the Holy Spirit. How many people believed the lies? The whole nation. You will also see similar stories of people whose lives were destroyed in this country by false accusation. As you read of them in my quotes, I urge you to research the stories for yourselves.

Job, the Bible called him the righteous man of the east. One thing Job said that I also strongly can relate to is recorded in Job. 3:25 *"For the thing which I greatly feared is come upon me, and that which I was afraid of is come unto me"* (Holy Bible, KJV)

Maybe it is because of my orientation as a Liberian. I thought that the people of America were superior to every human on earth, at least that's what we were made to believe. I felt inferior to the Americans even before I arrived here, it was not until later on that I began to understand that Americans or Liberians, we are all human beings created by the Lord God. But initially, I was overwhelmed by inferiority complex. That is why I identified with Job 3:25.

From the reading of the scripture, we now know that it was not because of any sin Job committed that brought the temptation on him, but the statement of his friends toward him made it sound as if it was his faults. In the same way in my case, the statement of the public toward me, behind my back, seems as though I am guilty of the countless accusations being labeled on me.

Listen to the statements from the friend of Job who heard of his plight and came to comfort him. Listen to the comforting words: "*Remember, I pray thee, who ever perished, being innocent? Or where were the righteous cut off? Even as I have seen, they that plow iniquity, and sow wickedness, reap the same" Job 4:7 and 8 Holy Bible (KJV)*. Comforting?

It's like I said earlier. I have not been questioned by anyone. All they are doing is whispering behind my back. And all those that are doing the whispering included law enforcement personnel. They all say I am guilty of their lies.

Could it be the reason why the Lord says in the book of Romans 8:28, "*And we know that all things work together for good to them that love God, to them who are the called according to his purpose.*" There are many things that we do not understand in the pathway of life. While we are often time victimized by these circumstances, we are unable to prevent them from occurring especially if the origin is divine, as in the case of righteous Job.

My introduction: I was born in Liberia, June 10, 1961, unto the union of Lewis and Fatu Shasha, in Japan's Town Pleemu clan. What seemed to be an endless civil war grape Liberia on December 24, 1989. Like many Liberians, I saw and experienced so many things, some of which I have already mentioned. I will tell you a little more when I mention my son.

In America, before moving to my own apartment, I became a member of the Columbus Baptist Temple, on Cleveland Avenue, now known as the Cross Road Baptist Church, in 2001. In 2002, the church commences construction work on a new building. The pastor at the time asked members for their time, their talent, and their treasure.

I told the pastor treasure I did not have, but time and talent I have, and that I will give. We commence the construction. I worked as a volunteer. It happened that I got home from work one morning, change my clothes, and went to work at the church construction site. Trinity Construction Company, who had the contract to build the church, contracted some masons to do the brickwork around the base of the building.

The temptation I'm faced with that led to the tarnishing of my reputation got its roots from here. It was my first time seeing any of the masons working. They commence the bricklaying in the back of the building near the mission's room.

# THE TEMPTATION

I knew all of the men of Trinity that worked on the project because I started working with them the very first day we commenced the project. As it was my habit, always when I got on the project site, I greeted all that were working, said thanks to them before going to ask the foreman for my assignment.

I really don't remember the day, but I arrived at the church around 9:00 a.m. Just as I began to say hi to the guys and thanked the bricklayers, one of the masons, an elderly white man, said to me, "Go back to your country. We don't want any foreigner here. Get out of here and go home, go back to your country." At that, one of the men working for Trinity, a black man who had worked on the project since the day we commenced, said to the mason, "He is with this church, he's a member and working as a volunteer."

"I don't care," the mason said to the black man. "Let him go back to his country." Talk about a mean old man; yes, he was the one. He was mean and very bitter toward me for no reason except that I was a foreigner. Before the day was over, a black SUV drove up at the construction site; the driver was a black man, the passenger was a white man, who took my picture. I then walk to the truck and asked, "Why did you take my picture?" The black man who was driving the SUV said to me, "You will see it in the papers tomorrow." I laughed and went back to work. I told the project supervisor, who I will name P, about it, but he said nothing. That day, while going home from work at the church, I stopped by at my relative's place, with whom I lived until I got my apartment.

I was told that a lady from the INS had called that day, wanting to know my status in the country. I made the comment, "They have my information, let them call my lawyer and asked him." The next day, I called my lawyer and asked him if he had received any called from the INS. No, he said, he then asked me why. I told him that a lady had called from the INS the day before, wanting to know my status. "Well, they will give me a call if they have any questions," my lawyer said.

From the day I arrived in this country, May11, 2001, until this day in 2002, I had no problems, and everything was fine for me and with me. But as of the day that my picture was taken while working at the church, or should I say until the day that the mason told me to go back to my home Country, things had never been the same. I began to notice so many things. I moved from 3085 Charlotte Drive, Columbus,

Ohio, where I lived with relative to my own apartment at 4336 Thornapple Circle West, Columbus, Ohio 43231, it was the tenth of May 2002. Few months after I moved, I got home from work one night, showered, and went to bed. Then came to me a vision that night. In the vision, I got home from work. As I got out off my car, I noticed across from my apartment there were a group of people conspiring against me. They all were looking at me intensively.

The vision passed. As I came through, I knew right away that something was to happen and that the facilitators were going to be mostly of a particular group of people. After the vision the next night, when I got home from work, I got a phone call from a lady at about 11:10-11:20 p.m. She said that she was calling from some department of safety, and that they were doing some survey, and that I have been chosen to participate.

(Illegal, I know. You do not call someone at that time of the night to conduct a survey. Suspicious? Yes.) As we talked, a sensation of deep awareness came over me. Even though I was seated at the top of the steps with the door and windows locked, I was made aware spiritually that my phone line was being wiretapped (monitored). I also saw the lady sitting in the apartment opposite mine. I saw her in the spirit. We talked for about thirty to forty minutes, after which I went into the bathroom to take my bath. As I lay down, I saw in a vision a man coming in to my apartment, pretending to be a telephone salesman. He was an undercover agent coming to assess my apartment. The way he sat down on the chair indicated to me that he was feeling the cushion to see if a gun was being kept in the chair.

When the vision passed, I knew right away that someone was coming to my apartment for that purpose. By the way, may I add here that from my boyhood until now I have never owned a gun, nor do I ever intend to own one.

Just as I saw it in the vision, the next day a man came to my apartment and introduced himself as a salesman from the phone company I was using at the time. "Can I come in?" he asked. "Yep, yep, come in," I said. Just as it was in the vision, he sat in the same spot, in the same chair and did exactly what had taken place in my vision. When he introduced himself, I was informed through a sentiment that I cannot explain that he was lying. We talked for a few minutes and then he left.

The next thing that I noticed was that the original occupants of the apartment opposite me and the one right behind me were relocated in the apartment complex. The new occupants moved in. Something very funny took place that caused me to laugh. The apartment directly opposite mine, the occupant cut an opening in the blinds of their bedroom window. They inserted in the opening a webcam that faces directly at my apartment, keeping a 24-7 watch on my apartment. That was not all.

They put a device in their apartment, which beamed at my front door so that every time I open my front door, the device will sound an alarm that sounded like a dog barking.

One of my neighbors also have similar device in place where I'm now living. Directly behind my apartment, the new renter also placed a webcam to the glass wall of their back door to enable them to monitor all that was going on in the back of my apartment. Also, a pole was erected right out front of my bedroom window which contains a high-tech camera mounted unto it. I then began to notice cars coming and parking at the end of the parking lot north of my apartment.

The drivers never got out. As I got in my car to go to work, they drove behind me until I reached the working place, and then they drove off. It was not a one-time occurrence but every day, both going to and from work, even when I went to church.

I must admit that fear took me, the reason being that here I am in a strange country for reason unknown to me at the time. I see people stalking me, stalking me everywhere I went. I was petrified. I then decided to do what I knew best. I went to the Lord, in prayers, to ask him for protection and to let me know what was happening. Three days into my prayers, I was informed in a vision of what will take place when the temptation was over. I was told that the temptation would last for twenty-nine days. I did not know what to make of the twenty-nine days because II Peter 3:8 says, "*But, beloved, be not ignorant of this one thing, that one day is with the Lord as a thousand years, and a thousand years as one day.* Also Psalms 90:4 says, "*For a thousand years in thy sight are but as yesterday when it is past, and as a watch in the night*" Holy Bible (KJV).

When I received this revelation, I did not stop my prayers. I continue my prayers. About seven days into my prayers, I saw three angels again in a night vision. The three of them surrounded me and held in their hand what looked like a Murom Curtin. They held it around me as I stood in the midst of them. Then one of them spoke to me, "No shame and disgrace will come to any one." As the night vision passed and I came through, I asked myself, "Why did he say what he said?" The reason is that I was the only one here at the time; my family was still in Liberia. So for him to say what he said, it left me wondering.

I did not get the answer to why this temptation was taking place from the spirit realm but from the physical realm. One thing that did take place was that I received a greater spiritual awareness.

By now fear was no longer a part of me, but before then there was a day when I thought of ending my life. I thought to myself I will get in my car and drive off, without paying any attention. I will run into a tree because if anything, I wanted only I alone to be involved. As I sat thinking of this thoughts, this overwhelming awareness came over me. In the awareness, the question was asked me: "What have you done that is of evil since you came to this country?" I said nothing. Then came another question: "Why are you trouble, and why are you worrying?" With those questions came a peace of mind.

As though what was happening to me was not enough, I lost my job, which was due to the expiration of my work permit. Since I was already working as a volunteer on the church project, I spoke with the owner of the company. "You wanted to pay me when I started working on the church project, to which I said no. It is because I promised to used my talent for God. But I lost my job today because my work permit expired."

The owner of the company then asked me, "What do you want me to do?" "To pay me when I work to enable me pay my rent and my car note." "How much do you want me to pay you?" he asked me. I said, "$10 per hour." "Go to work, Emmett," the owner said.

I begin taking pay from Trinity the last two weeks of October 2002 until January of 2003. Because I was being paid, I could no longer work at my church only but went wherever Trinity had a project. By the end of January my work permit was renewed. I got back my old job, with the same company. I then told the owner of Trinity, "Thanks for the three months of pay, and that I am going back to be a volunteer on the church project."

Still in 2002 while fully working for Trinity, I was transferred to work on Mock Road on another church building an, Apostolic Church. When it came to working, I always like to get to work on time. We started work by 7:30 a.m. to 4:00 p.m. It happened that on this Friday, the boss had said that we were not starting work until 9:00 a.m. Saturday morning. I did not get the message. I went to work the same usual time Saturday morning. I arrived at the church at 7:00 a.m. normally few minutes after others began arriving, but I waited until 8:00 a.m. When no one came, I used the pay phone located opposite the church compound in the yard of a convenience store to call the owner of Trinity. He then informed me that we were not starting job until 9:00 a.m. While on the pay phone with my boss, I saw a black man who appeared to be homeless. He had just come from checking out the trash container. He walked to the convenience store and stood by the entrance, looking toward me. By the time I got done talking and walked back across the road to my car, I saw him enter the store. Before long, two police cars took up position on opposite ends of the road facing toward each other.

I then asked myself why were they here, the police that is. Then I was made to understand that the homeless man had told the store owner that the black man sitting across the road in the Chevrolet was on the phone and he have an accent. I don't know what he was saying, but it's like he's awaiting some people. It was with that information that the store owner called the police.

I arrived at the job site at 7:00 a.m. By 8:00 a.m., I called the boss. Well, "I have been here all this time, I will just wait," I thought to myself. The police cars remain in position until the others workers came to work. We worked from 9:00 a.m.-12:00 noon. As we got off work, the police cars also drove off. Blocked numbers began calling my home like every thirty to forty-five minutes.

The moment I picked up a signer in my spirit that something wrong was occurring somewhere in the city. The next moment, my phone will ring. The security called to see if I was home. It was revealed to me that even though I am wearing clothes, those that were following me were able to see my nakedness because of the special glass they were using. I was then informed that everywhere I turn, I was going to be monitored by air, land, and phone.

On December 26, 2002, I told someone that I noticed people following me. They then asked me why. I said I don't know. They advised me to go and report the matter to the police. That same day, I went to the police substation on Morse Road and Karl Road and reported the matter to the police—that people were following me (stalking). The officer took down my name and my complain and said that they were going to look into it. After I made the report to the police substation, I went to work that night. While at work, I saw in a vision a police car taking up position. I was made to understand that the police car taking up position was not there to follow me, rather it was there because of the report I made.

As I exited the building, I looked to where I had seen the police car in the vision. There it was, only that it was not the red, white, and blue car; it was an undercover brown bus. After a while of covering me, when they realized that there were no bad persons stalking me rather it was another department of law enforcement, they stopped coming.

I wanted to know which branch of the government was stalking me. I went back into prayers before the week was over. While still in prayers, I went to help one of the ladies from the church move her things. While working, she said to me, "You be careful and behave yourself. I heard from the horse's mouth that the Department of Homeland Security is watching your every move." I smiled and said, "Let them go ahead."

I got the answer that I wanted, but was she willing to go with me to court and testify. The answer was no. I thought to myself, "How can you put an end to rumors if no one is willing to speak out?" The following week, I was with another person from the church who said to me, "You know, you have a very good testimony in the church. You be careful because you can never tell who's watching you." At that I said, "Let them go ahead and watch because I have nothing to hide."

It was in that time that I heard about Prepay Legal. While going through their membership guide, there was something very interesting on page page 7 that grabbed my attention. It was the fourth paragraph under the heading "Use Your Membership!"

**THE BEST WAY TO REALIZE THE VALUE OF YOUR MEMBERSHIP IS TO USE IT! IT MIGHT SEEM EASIER TO TAKE MATTERS INTO YOUR OWN HANDS OR TO SIMPLY IGNORE A PROBLEM AND HOPE IT GOES AWAY-BUT HAVING A PRE-PAID PLAN MEANS YOU NO LONGER HAVE TO HANDLE THINGS THIS WAY!**

# PRE-PAID LEGAL

I was fascinated by the statement and thought to myself that if I became a member of these people, I'm sure they will be able to help me get to the bottom of what is happening. Boy, was I wrong because when the time came when I expected them to use the law on my side, they just didn't do it. My expectation was that I will inform them of what is happening, they will in turn go to the court and put forth my cause and have the court called the DHS to show cause why are they doing what they are doing to me. I wrote Pre Paid Legal concerning the matter. When I did not hear from them, I then gave them a call. I spoke with one of their attorney who asked me who or what branch of the government was stalking me, is it Federal or local? Not knowing the difference, I said local. He then asked me which department. I told him it was the Department of Homeland Security. He then said that it was federal. After a while, I got a letter from them, which totally did not represent the quotation I gave from page 7 of their membership guide. I will include in this book the letter that I wrote to them and also the response they sent me.

According to their reply, they said that "we have determined that there is no issue of the law for us to address. Therefore, as attorneys, we are unable to offer any assistance or legal solution to your situation." Reading this quote, does it not sound contradicting from their membership guide, *"It might seem easier to take matters into your own hands or to simply ignore a problem and hope it goes away—but having a Pre Paid Legal plan means you no longer have to handle things this way"*

Is it that there is no issue of the law for them to address, or the real issue is that I am a Black African with an accent? Besides, who am I to say that a federal agency of the government is stalking me?

With all due respect to the attorneys of Pre-Paid, I think that there are so many things in the law, things of which you could address but failed to do so. I guess you did it with the hope that something bad will happen to me, then you will come in; or perhaps I will be kicked out of the country, then you will not have to deal with me anymore. Yet you are still taking money from my account. In what way then will you be able to assist me legally? Let me add, if that was your thinking, well you are wrong because I am here to stay. Or perhaps you thought that there was no possibility that the government could offend someone for which you will be called upon to protect the rights of the innocent. Or maybe the cameras were not rolling for people to see you guys on TV. Normally, that's the time people pretend to have the innocents at heart. Check the Internet for yourselves. The records are there for all to read. See how many Americans' lives have been destroyed because of the very complain that I am making today, yet you say that there is nothing in the law. Please.

According to you, the attorneys of Pre-Paid, you said, "We have determined that there is no issue of the law for us to address." Excuse me. Is the Declaration of Independence of the United State of America still holding true to its value today as it did in the days of old when it was first adopted? If it does, then what about this clause: *"We hold these Truths to be self-evident, that all men are created equal, that they are endowed by their Creator with certain unalienable Rights, that among these are Life, Liberty, and the pursuit of Happiness"*? Perhaps you might argue and say that it has nothing to do with my concern being raised. When it comes to the protection of one's freedom, it does. It is the right of all man as embedded in the Declaration of Independence of this nation of which I am a citizen—to live in peace with a peace of mind.

If you still hold on to your argument, that it is the Declaration of Independence, well, let's invoke the first five amendments to the constitution. If what I'm saying were not occurring on a daily basis in this nation, then you could say that I am insane. But you see it happening, and when you are called upon to protect the ones whom you claim to represent, you downplay them by saying, "There is no issue of the law to address." I have a problem with that, but that's my opinion. "Who cares?" some will say.

Perhaps, the noble attorneys of Pre-Paid Legal would say that they did not know where to start. Well, I sent them copies of the letters that I wrote to various statesmen. I believe that my letter to pre-paid legal raising my concern along with the letters I sent to the statesmen which were never replied could have started some proceeding. If there were anyone who knew the law, it should have been pre-paid legal. For them to say what they said in their reply to me is just beyond me. I will quote in this book finding made by scholars on the conviction of innocent people in this nation. Perhaps it will help the broad audiences reading this book to understand what I am saying.

As I will mention later for you to see, of the many who lives were defamed by the system only to come back later to say we are sorry it was a mistake, well, those people were not privileged to see it coming. But when it came upon them, I bet they pleaded their guts out, hoping that someone would have heard their earnest cry for justice, but it all fell on deaf ears. It's like what the scholars of a research team said that, "most wrongful convictions resulted from a combination of errors. The mean case, in more than half of the cases—was eyewitness misidentification overzealous prosecutor . . ." (reseachnews.OSU.edu/archive/ronhuff.htm).

I can't help but mention here over and over, as you read, you notice me saying that an overwhelming sentiment came over me, and then I became aware or I was informed. This is how it happened: If you are a Christian or maybe you are just a reader, in reading the Holy Bible, the book of 1 Corinthians 12, you will see that there are diversities of spiritual gifts, at the most for me to apprehends these awareness of the information been given to me one of these gift comes into play.

Before the establishment of Sound Doctrine, while still with Baptist Temple, I received the vision of a man, a member of the church, that he was really eyeing me. I did something stupid one Sunday. I say stupid because I spoke without obtaining permission first, something I should not have done. However, the pastor expressed his dissatisfaction. I apologized and it was done. On this particular Sunday, I waited until the pastor got through with his message. As he walked down from the pulpit, I then mounted the pulpit and said, "I believe strongly that I am a victim of mistaken identity. There are people stalking me for no apparent reason. I'm appealing to them to please leave me alone."

After I made the statement and walked outside, the very man who was revealed to me as having his eyes on me came to me and mentioned the name of a man and asked me if I knew the man. It was my first time hearing that name, and so I replied, "No, I don't know him." He then said to me, "Are you not a Nigerian?" I said, "No, I am a born Liberian." "But all of you look alike." I said no to him. "I am a Liberian, and I look like myself." By then I was only a legal alien, living here, I was not a permanent resident yet.

The Sunday that I made the statement in the church "of me being a victim of mistaken identity," a family in the church that were home-schooling their children had spoken with me and my wife of how they wanted to help our son with tutoring. We agreed, but everything changed that Sunday. The following Monday, I got a call from the mother who is of that family, informing me that they will not be able to do the tutoring for my son. I asked why, and she said, "Oh something just came up, that's why." I said thanks, and that was the end, knowing already the reason why she said that. I did not see it as important to warrant me to pray in order to find out why. My son was in middle school by then.

While I have not served in public office, I have lived in this nation as a peaceful, law-abiding alien; a peaceful, law-abiding permanent resident. And now as a citizen, I ask God that I remain humble and continue to live as a peaceful, law-abiding citizen. Even though I am not a Muslim, I applaud Senator John Mccain in his stand as he spoke out for the wife of former Senator Anthony Weiner. People should not be tarnishing the reputation of others to seek political favor, or like in my case to keep themselves on a job by making up lies about people and destroying their reputation. It's my hope that someone will speak out concerning my plight after reading my book.

Apart from writing to pre-paid legal as I mentioned earlier, I also wrote to permanent people in the State of Ohio. All the letters that I wrote will be published in this book. As I was saying, that I wrote to permanent people in this state with the hope that they will use their good offices and position to stop the madness of the Department of Homeland Security from making a grave mistake by destroying the life of an innocent person. But all of my appeal was to no avail.

The first person I wrote was His Excellency Honorable Ted Strickland; then governor elect of the State of Ohio. The letter was dated December 6, 2006. Even though the letter was sent by certified mail, I received no reply. I also did a follow-up with an e-mail but got no reply.

The second letter that I wrote was to the attorney general of the State of Ohio, Richard Cordray. His letter was dated June 8, 2009. I received no written reply, but a phone called from an office staff who told me that the attorney general of the State of Ohio did not have jurisdiction over the place where I lived (4167 Arbury Ln, Columbus, Oh 43224 Franklin County).

Tell that to the child that is born today, not to me. It was like saying that the governor of Ohio has no jurisdiction over Franklin County, even though the site of governess is in Columbus, which is in Franklin County. Could that be true? You decide. There is a saying that says wonders shall never end. While reading the manuscript of this book, our church received a letter from the attorney general's office. The letter was saying to the fact that "based on statutory authority," the church should respond to the questions that were provided on the enclosed questionnaire. The letter was dated August 9, 2012. I find it very interesting to know today that the attorney general's office has statutory authority over our church. While our congregation meets for regular worship service in the youth building of the Cross Road Baptist Church, my home address is still used for the church since we are still in the process of obtaining a building of our own, and it was my home address that was used to register the church. It is this same address that the former attorney general's office of the State of Ohio said that they had no jurisdiction over, when I wrote to his office asking for assistance in defense of my reputation. Double standard or what? As you read, you decide. One interesting thing that did happen was that a particular car that I mentioned in my observation, which was attached to the attorney general's letter, was pulled back from aggressive stalking. I guess you can say they knew that his cover was now uncovered.

On the same day, June 8, 2009, I also wrote to Dr. Leroy Z. Boikai, who was servicing in the capacity as president of the Liberian community in Columbus. Even though he did not reply to my letter, he told me to just forget about it. It is one thing to tell someone "I share your pains," and it is another thing to say "I am having this pain that just wouldn't go away."

On the same day still, June 8, 2009, I wrote to Maguire & Schneider L.L.P, (Pre-Paid), my legal reprehensive. In their reply, they basically told me that I had no case.

Tell that to the innocent victim project that are unearthing almost daily cases of people that were falsely accused of crimes they did not commit and were found guilty in the court of law and then thrown into prison.

Lastly, I wrote to His Excellency Honorable Rob Portmen, senator of the United States, a senator from Ohio. His letter was dated October 24, 2011. He still have yet to respond to my letter.

Is it really justice for all? The "One Nation, Under God, Indivisible with Liberty and Justice for all," does it still hold true? What about the Constitution, the ideals of self-governance, "We the people of the United States, in order to form a more perfect Union, establish, Justice, insure domestic Tranquility, provide for the common defense, promote the general Welfare, and secure the Blessings of Liberty to ourselves and our Posterity, do ordain and establish this Constitution for the United States of America." "Domestic Tranquility." I believe that the Constitution of the land still stands, but is it being ahead to is the question.

Even though you will read it in my letters to the various statesmen, but let me mention what my concern is, for which I am sitting down to write the book, it is to let the world to know what the plight is that I am confronted with that is destroying my reputation.

Like I mentioned earlier, my life was going fine until the mason said to me, "Go back home to your country. We do not want any foreigner here," followed by the black SUV coming on the church compound and my picture being taken by the passenger and then the call from the INS. After all these scenarios, the next thing that I noticed was that *I was now being accused of being a Nigerian, a Muslim, a murderer, and a thief!* All these allegations are false, baseless, misleading, and only gear on tarnishing my reputation, to which for the most part it had succeeded to some extent.

My letters, as you will read, to these local and federal leaders were written with the hope that these leaders were going to allow justice, transparency, and wisdom to play out its course in the spirit of truthfulness. Rather, they decided to keep silence and turn a blind eye and a deaf ear to an earnest cry for justice.

Going to court for me was an option, but without someone to testify for the crime being committed against me, that would have been a tough nut to crack. That's why these letters were written. On the side of justice, truth, and human's right, no one is willing to come out to speak.

Not that it is not known of the people in the system. If it will be fixed, it had to start from somewhere, perhaps people of good will that have the hearts of God, can look beyond the public acceptance of the lies, and take a stand for justice. As was done by Senator McCain and others when they spoke out for the reputation of the former senator's wife.

I chose the plight of Joseph in Egypt and Job, the righteous man of the east who feared God, because they both experienced interesting situations similar to what I am going through. By all accounts, these two biblical characters were guilty in the eyes of the public even though they had committed no crime. I mentioned earlier that no law enforcement personnel had spoken to me nor have I gone to court, yet I have been found guilty by the DHS and the public in general for things I did not do and things that I have no idea about.

One can really not blame the public because they are carrying around the lies, false rumors, and character assassination which are fed to them by the Department of Homeland Security. Do you think that I am the first? Of course not. I will not give their names because I do not have their permission; I will only use the initials of these people. In a section of this book, I will mention their stories.

I spoke of going to the police substation located at the intersection of Morse Road and Karl Road in Columbus, Ohio, to make a formal complaint of people stalking me. That was December 26, 2002. In 2008, I went back to the same substation to request for a police report regarding my complaint in 2002. I was then informed by the officer I met that I had to go downtown to the Columbus Division of Police to obtain a report.

I went to the CDP that same day to request a copy of the police report; the lady I spoke with told me to hold on while she went to check and that she will be right back. Few minutes after she left, an overwhelming sentiment of awareness came over me. Even though I was standing at the counter waiting for the lady who was clearly out of view, I heard the voice of a man in my spirit talking with the lady. "Oh my gosh," she said. "This is the guy we are monitoring." "We could take him now," the man said. "What will you charge him with?" the lady asked. At that point, the lady came back to the counter where I was waiting for her. She said to me, "We do not have any record of that complaint, only the one for the telephone harassment." I told her to give me a copy of that and then I left the division and headed home. Of course she was lying. I will also place the copy in this book.

Back in 2004, I went to the post office to send some document to my lawyer. I sat in my car at the post office, putting all of the papers together. By the time I was done, an overwhelming sentiment of fear came over me. I asked what it was all about; the fear was as strong as the one that I felt back in Liberia on December 25, 1990. Right there and then, I sunk down in my spirit to see my surrounding. In the spirit, I saw men taking up position in and outside of the post office.

Their commander was wearing a short jeans pain about knee-length. He weighed about 225 to 235 lbs. He was black and had a tattoo of the American eagle on his right arm. To alert the others when I entered the post office, the code was "Look what we have got here!"

Upon receiving this information, I got out of my car and walked into the post office. Everything was just as I had seen it in the spirit. After mailing the document, which was later opened by them after I left, I was compelled by a force beyond me, which I believe was the Spirit of God, to walk very slow, something which I don't normally do. I could have been shot that very day for nothing.

The instruction to the men that were posted was that if I came out of the building walking fast or running, I should be shot. I walked as slow as I could until I reached my car. I got into my car and drove home.

Not too long after that, I called my wife who was still in Liberia. My wife and I were arguing about something. When we got done talking and said bye to one another, just as I put down the phone, it rang. I picked up the phone. "Hello," I said. The voice on the other end was that of a man who said to me, "So you think that you are the man at home! Right! Right! We will see to that." He then dropped the phone.

Let me mention that it was a local call. From what I gathered from this man who called, he was listening to my wife and I talking, and he was very angry with me for no reason. It was my wife I was talking with, and this man, I believe, even had the audacity to harm me if he had been standing near me, for no apparent reason, as though he had never had an argument with his wife—that is if he was married, to a woman. I hope you will understand when I said to stop the madness of the DHS. It is because of the rumors, lies, and character assassination being perpetuated against me that is causing all these things to occur.

In 2003, I made a TV appearance on channel 4 NBC-NEWS. According to the facilitators, it was to inform the world of the plight of my family that were still in Liberia. The interview was conducted by one Mandry Dryer. At the end of the interview, her cameraman did something that is not typical for a cameraman to do to an interviewee except if that person was a criminal. He made a 360-degree shot around my head, recording every detail of my head and upper body, to the point that Mandry asked him, "Do you really have to do that?" The whole interview became suspicious.

The whole idea of the interview looked good to me at first until I got the detail of it from the spirit realm.

The revelation I got was this: while the revelation came to me from the spirit realm what I'm about to explain took place in the physical realm. Meaning that it really did happen in real life. I went to work one day. At that time, the company had a red van. One of the staff and I took the consumers out for a van ride. I was seated in the front sit of the van, on the passenger side. As we crossed Cleveland Avenue heading west into Fuji Road, the car of the then pastor of Columbus Baptist Temple was at the red light. It was a white open-top Corvette. Both he and his son were in the car. I called out to the pastor's son by name and waved at him; he also waved back.

The following Sunday at church, the pastor's son asked me, "How did you come to this country?" Mind you, he was asking me this question in 2003, I became a member of the church in 2001, I even spent 2001 Christmas at their home. Of the many things we talked about before, never did he ask me such question. I asked him, "What do you mean by how did I get here?" I then said to him by plane. The next thing then was the pastor saying to me, "Come in your best outfit on Sunday. A television team is coming to church to conduct an interview with you concerning your family."

It sounded very good to me that by doing so, the world will get to know the plight of my family who was still in Liberia, facing what became known in Liberia as war, war three. My family suffered so many things during this particular war. I was in Liberia during the war of Octopus in 1992. I was also there during the war of April 6, 1996, but from what I was told, the war of 2003 was the dirtiest of all. It was also during this war that my eldest son was captured by one of the warring factions. I will publish in this book a fact sheet of the organization that was trying to contact my family to help rescue them out of Liberia. (1989-1996, first civil war; 1997-2003, second civil war; 2003, post-Taylor ceasefire).

# CENTER FOR REFORM

*Dedicated to educating and assisting the public in constructive citizenship and humanitarian activities*

## MISSION TO LIBERIA FACT SHEET

## ABDUCTION OF ZUBAH SHASHA

- Zubah Shasha was abducted by the rebel group LURD – Liberians United for the Restoration of Democracy on Saturday July 26, 2003 while the Shasha family was fleeing the fighting.

- Zubah Shasha will now face the "training" program of LURD. Africans call this "recruitment" but the reality is that it is torture pure and simple.

- Zubah will be beaten until one of two things happen:
  - He agrees to fight for LURD and do what he is told
  - He dies

- If he survives he will be placed with "veterans"
  - LURD members who have a couple of months of survival under their belt

- Zubah will be given a weapon and will be expected to fight.
  - He will not receive training as a soldier.
  - He will not be fighting for an ideology or a well-defined cause.

- Zubah Shasha will be placed on the front lines of whatever battle is handy; he will not have any fighting skills.
  - He will most likely not even be trained in how to properly aim his weapon.
  - He will simply be fodder in the senseless violence that is gripping Liberia.

- Zubah Shasha faces possible death before we can find him.

- If LURD can find the Shasha family, they will be killed.

  - Zubah's younger brother, Joshua Moses Shasha age 11 would be taken to fight for the rebels.

# LURD FACTS

- Known as LURD – Liberians United for the Restoration of Democracy
- Based in Liberia and Guinea
- Command and Control located in Guinea
- Leadership of LURD receives protection from the Presidential Guard of Guinea
- Receives supplies from the government of Guinea
  - Ammunition
  - Weapons
  - Transportation and Vehicles
  - Fuel, Food and other supplies

CONTACT AND DONATION INFORMATION:

Center for Reform
P.O. Box 77286
Washington, DC 20013
866-278-3055
tranquility@uscfr.com

Pastor Victor Jungkurth
Columbus Baptist Temple
5075 Cleveland Ave.
Columbus, Ohio 43231
614-895-5683

# CENTER FOR REFORM

*Dedicated to educating and assisting the public in constructive citizenship and humanitarian activities*

## MISSION TO LIBERIA FACT SHEET

- The Center for Reform is currently implementing emergency activities to provide humanitarian support to Liberia.

- Organized under the general mission and vision of the Campaign for Tranquility.

- The Campaign for Tranquility has as its' core mission to promote non-violence and positive values that will assist citizens in developing a healthy environment for community development and growth.

- While the Campaign for Tranquility is still in its infancy, the Center for Reform feels that the needs of the People of Liberia cannot be ignored.

## WHY LIBERIA?

- Mission to Liberia is being conducted in cooperation with the Columbus Baptist Temple

- In November of 2002, the Columbus Baptist Temple seeking assistance with the immigration case (political asylum) of Mr. Emmett Shasha contacted the Center for Reform.

- The Center for Reform has in the past successfully advocated on behalf of individuals in immigration proceedings (usually asylum cases) and has originated and managed extraction of families at risk from hostile situations in the Middle East and Africa.

- The Center for Reform also advocates for human and civil rights in cases around the world.

# THE IMPORTANCE OF THIS PROJECT

- Implemented as a part of the overall vision and mission of the Campaign for Tranquility, Mission to Liberia will mark the first broad cooperation of African countries with a Non Profit Organization for a specific humanitarian mission.

- Without immediate action the body count will continue to rise.

- Recently bodies of victims were stacked in front of the US Embassy in Monrovia and are the direct result of violence; all of the victims were killed in the recent attacks.

- The body count promises to grow much larger without proactive measures. The cause will not be gunfire or explosion but malnutrition and disease.

- For every victim of direct violence there are hundreds who will die from the more silent killers of hunger and disease without intervention.

- Currently it is estimated that over 300 people per day are dying from cholera in Monrovia.

- Successful operation of this project will allow the Center for Reform and other humanitarian organizations to move into Liberia at the earliest possible date with humanitarian projects including a Campaign for Tranquility designed specifically for post war recovery.

# DEVELOPING A SUPPLY-CHAIN FOR LIFE

## AN INTERIM LIFELINE

- Current efforts are underway to establish of a supply chain to facilitate the delivery of medicines and other supplies targeted for those who are suffering the most.

- The Center is working on a cooperative basis to develop supply lines for the delivery of humanitarian supplies under the protection of peacekeepers while the more traditional methods of delivery are reestablished.

- Food and medicine supplies are running low in Monrovia.

- The Center for Reform is currently contacting food brokers and corporations in search of donated food items that can be transported to Liberia in an effective manner to reduce hunger and suffering. Similar requests are also being made for pharmaceuticals.

- In particular the Center is actively searching for freeze dried and evaporated products such as milk and eggs to supply protein into the diet of recipients and to enhance the ability to feed as many people as possible.

- Currently there are a number of humanitarian programs operating with very little food reserves. Liberian refugees are lining up to receive one spoonful of rice. Food is scarce and the harsh reality for the children of Liberia is that when it is gone they go hungry until more food can be located.

# SOUND DOCTRINE FIRST SERVICE

The pastor and I had no former discussion before this day. It was shocking and surprising when he told me, but because I wanted the world to know about my family's plight I agreed to do the interview. I could have refused, but doing so would have made him think that I had something to hide. Even though I did not know his motive then, yet I accepted in good faith. I came to church and did the interview that Sunday The real reason for the TV interview was not to tell the world about my family's plight; if it was so, it could have taken place in 2001 when I became a member of the church.

It was because his son saw me in the van with a group of men. Of course the consumer that I worked with are mostly men. From there a negative image of me was drawn in their mind. "Well, let's get him on TV," they thought to themselves. "Perhaps someone will recognize him as being some evil guy and then the authority can nab him." By then the rumors fabricated against me by the DHS were in its fullness.

I asked the then pastor for a copy of the interview; he told me that he could not give it to me because he was sending it somewhere. "Where?" I asked. "Somewhere," he replied. I never got a copy of the interview from him. When we started the ministry, we invited a lot of people to our first service. This service took place in the basement of our home. Nine persons were in attendance.

Of the many people we invited, one of the ladies was an informant. I really did not know at the time, but the night before the service, I saw in the vision of the night a police car driven by a woman that came to the service. At the passing of the vision, I waited the next day to see it unfold. Of all the people that came to the service, no one parked in the spot where the police car was parked in the vision. Just before the service started, a white car drove in and parked right on the spot; this white car was also driven by a lady.

Remember how I said earlier that on the twenty-six of December 2002, how I went to the police substation at the intersection of Morse Road and Karl Road junction and reported that people were stalking me, and the police officer said that they were going to look into it, and how that in a vision of the night I saw a police car come to take up position? And that just how I have seen it in the vision; it was so the next day, only that it was an undercover brown bus and not the red, white, and blue car. Well, this is what is taking place here in this vision.

By the way, this lady was the last to come. When we commenced the service, she left for the rest room, it was not to use it but to turn on the devise she was carrying under her clothes to send out every word that was to be spoken doing the service. It's like having a radio or TV crude transmitting on events as it takes place. After that service, she never came back again, not that she did not like the service, but she did not like the idea of being used as a puppet against someone whom she knew in her spirit that was being destroyed for nothing. That was the information given to me from the spirit realm.

People who say the true society tend to downplay them, but they will give credence to those that tell lies against others, accusing them for things they know nothing about. When I wrote to those statesmen, I told them in my letters that I will be willing to meet with them to discuss my letter. I even said in the letters that if they could not meet with me because of their busy schedule, I could meet with their representative.

I went on to tell them that I will be and am still willing to take a polygraph exam to prove my innocence. Did they read my letter with understanding? I think not. If it were so, they would have taken some actions. What I think happened was that upon the receipt of my letter, they might have instructed their office staff to contact the various securities apparatus to see if they can get that guy (that will be me) off the street so that they will not have to receive any more of such letters.

I wrote in my letters to those statesmen a word of truth to prove my innocence. They were not interested in hearing or seeing me most of all. I believe strongly that in their heart of hearts, they shared the same view as that of the mason who said "We do not want any foreigner here."

Who really owns this land anyway? Is it the American Indians who were met here by the Europeans that came here? Did I say come here? Yep, I did say that, or is it owned by the sons of both of them or all of the people who made it here? But who really owns this land? In my quest to get an answer I really did not have to do too much of a digging of who the real owner of the land is. Permit me to share with you my findings.

*"The earth is the LORD'S and the fullness thereof; the world, and they that dwell therein"* (Psalms 24:1) I being a son of my Heavenly Father that owns this land, how then can you tell me to leave? I will try to understand them on one ground, which is this that "I am in the world, but I am not of this world." Even as my savior, who gives his life for me, came in the world, but he was not of the world. There will come a day when

my Heavenly Father will call me home, from labor to rest. Until then, I remain a Liberian-born and a citizen of the USA.

All they were interested in is the rubbish being put forth by the DHS, which is deem on destroying my character by continually spreading their lies, false allegations, and character assassination. Like I said, they gave credence to those that told lies, misleading the nation to go to a senseless war, there spending billions of our taxes and losing thousands of precious lives of the sons and daughters of this land.

While can't they hear the cries for justice of those that are right under their feet and give them the liberty they are yearning for as encored in our sacred document of this nation. I will give you a scenario where our Lord alluded the thinking faculty of those who were elected by the people to seek the interest and well-being of the people; but to the contrary, once the oaths of office were taken, it became a different story.

There are things of yesterday that I find so interesting; it is how the events of yesterday fit in the affairs of today's life.

Our Lord Jesus Christ asked a question in Luke 7:31-32, "*And the Lord said, Whereunto then shall I liken the men of this generation? And to what are they like? They are like unto children sitting in the marketplace, and calling one to another, and saying, We have piped unto you, and ye have not dance; we have mourned to you and ye have not wept*" Holy Bible (KJV)

The question asked here by the Lord to which he also proceeded to give the answer also takes my mind back to Luke 3:14, "*And the soldiers likewise demanded of him, saying, And what shall we do? And he said unto them, Do violence to no man, neither accuse any falsely*" Holy Bible (KJV). As if they knew not what to do, they demanded of him, saying, "And what shall we do?" Why? asked John. He was not their commanding officer, yet he gave them a definitive answer, "Do violence to no man, neither accuse any falsely . . ." Did they really listen? I think not, reason being that few days later, he was arrested. Maybe not by the same group, but they were soldiers regardless, and then he was killed. (Do violence to no man.)

The soldiers that went to see John yesterday can be compared to that of the security establishment of our time. I am not a security personnel, but I believe that at the end of all of their training, before being placed on the streets or given an assignment, these people take an oath to protect life and property. Be it CIA, FBI, NSA, IP, CID, SU, etc. But rather than upholding the oath to protect life, they are sometimes the very first to destroy it. They are involved in the business of accusing people falsely.

Don't take my word for it, not that I do not stand by the wordings of this book. What I mean is that the source of information is at your fingertip; just go to the

Internet. If you are one person who doesn't listen to current events, there you will see volume of information on your fellow countrymen whose lives were destroyed by the system.

Dozens upon dozens of people, people who are wrongfully convicted in America—I am not talking about some third world country! I am talking about the United States of America. Where is the justice for all? While watching the documentary on the Mark of the Beast which was done by the 'Jack Van Impe Ministry'. In it I saw and heard a man say, "At first it used to be 'innocent till proven guilty,' now it is the other way around. It's now 'guilty till proven innocent.'"

# IT CAN HAPPEN TO ANYBODY

How true are his words. Until you are victimized by these circumstance you highly regard them as being truth, but they are. Oh, Lest I forget to mention this scenario: It took place in Liberia in 1989, at the time when the civil war was heating up. An old friend of mine who was also an army personnel came to our provision shop one evening to buy goods; He told me of how some of his fellow soldiers were going around looting things and killing innocent people, alleging that they were rebels or rebels sympathizers.

My response to him was "The solders knew whom to do it to." At that, he said, "No my son, they can do it to anybody, and there's nothing you can do about it." Foolish of me to answer him the way I did. Those words of his were something that will prove to be true not only in Liberia but in the United States as well.

About a week after my army friend made that revelation known to me, I left sinkor old road where I lived to travel to Barnersville Estate to see my aunt. I took a dozen of lunchmeat and other provision from our shop to give them to my aunt. At that time, the only cars running were all military, so if you were not a military personnel and you wanted to go from point A to point B, you had to walk. That day I walked for about five hours, going through one checkpoint after another; my bag was inspected at every checkpoint, and I was given permission to move on.

About quarter of a mile from my aunt's apartment, I met an army major with two bodyguards. One of the guards was very aggressive. He took my bag from me and threatened to kill me. As the army major and I talked, trying to explain to him that I was taking the things to my aunt, his bodyguard hit me in the middle of my back with the gun he had in his hand. The only thing that stopped them from killing me was the grace of God. That was done meanly to prove to me what the old army man, my friend, said. That "they can do it to anybody and there's nothing you can do about it." As you read this book, do not say to yourselves, "Oh, that just can't happen to me." No, don't say that because you could be the very next victim; maybe not you, but one of your relatives. It can happen to anybody.

As I write this book, it is now that I am beginning to understand what the mason said to me: "Go back home to your country. We do not want a foreigner here." I am now beginning to understand as the police chief in Arizona tried to enforce immigration laws. I can't help but ask myself, "Is it true patriotism or mere ignorance?" As said by the head of a private investigating firm whom I spoke with some time ago, "Most of the time, some of these things are mere ignorance."

As the immigration debate raged on, I heard a US congressman say, "If you live in Arizona, if your skin color is brown, and you had an accent, you are a suspect." I think his comment goes for Ohio as well. Even though he spoke not against immigrants, but the plight which they were facing.

I heard in the corridor of my surroundings, on the news, and from watching the TV, movies, and documentaries that if you were black in America, you were unfortunate. What that means is that you were born on the wrong side of the equator. Being black a foreigner with an accent meant that you were dirt. Not only that but you were born on the other side of the equator, and that you were also doomed for hell.

There isn't a day that goes by without my name being dragged in the mud, my reputation destroyed. I now understand why. Even though I have committed no crime in this nation, the Department of Homeland Security have not stopped trying to place a crime on my head. There is a device that is suspended in midair in the back of my house. It looks almost pink in color, it's shaped like a jellyfish, it has what looked like silk net attached to it, but you cannot see it with the naked eye. I will also try to include a picture of the object in the book along with the letters that I wrote to the various statesmen. On three occasions, they had helicopter hovering for my sake, on one of such occasions, I went to meet with my lawyer for an appointment. The helicopter came so close to the building until even my lawyer was afraid that the helicopter was going to crash in to the building. That was how close it was. I sat still and watched them. We could see each other because the wall of the building was glass. They looked at me and I looked back at them. I guess they were expecting me to get out of the building and run. With all that they have done to me, they still don't want to leave me alone.

One time they made a very and highly significant airplane pass over my house to scan our home. The magnetic wave was so intense that one could almost feel the wave penetrating their body. I knew what was going on but said nothing to my family.

On many occasions, police cruiser were dispatched to my location not upon my request but with the hope that I will be involved in some negativities for which I could be apprehended. Even though sometimes they used the code "bishop" or "the prophet" when referring to me, yet they refuse to accept that I am a Christian. Not only that I am a Christian but that I am a pastor. I have been privileged to see them clearly in the spirit as they walked to spread these false allegations against me.

I will go to the store to buy. While looking around for things to buy, sometimes they will call the store security or at times they will come in the store and talk with one of the store managers or the security, alerting them of my presence in the store and that they should keep an eye on me. They treat me as though I am a hard-core criminal.

These false accusations, spreading of false rumors coupled with character assassination of me on the part of the Department of Homeland Security I believe strongly play a part in me losing my employment with the Forum At Knightsbridge. I was employed March 26, 2010, and was terminated March 25, 2012. Right after I got employed, it wasn't long when some of my co-workers began throwing hints at me.

Referring to my wife, on one occasion, one of my co-workers said, "We heard about her husband. It is only now that we have seen you." "What is that supposed to mean?" I asked my co-worker. Oh, no! And then she walked out. I did the very best I could to ignore their hints. I did my job to the best of my ability, to the point that almost all the residents whom I work with got to know me by my name personally. I work with such efficiency and management was amazed. There was a change in management at the facility when the new leader took over. A precious white lady who was the big boss called me in the office of the director of nursing one day. She asked me for my secret. "What secret?" I asked. "You know, what is it that you are doing around here that makes all of the residents want you to attend to them?"

"Well," I told her, "when I come to work, I do not work as unto man, I do my work as unto God. In all my days of working, there's one thing which I did not do. It was to keep quiet on issues especially when it pertains to the residents for whom I was rendering service."

I spoke about every issue. Because of my outspokenness, many of the bosses did not like that. To make matters worse were the lies that were being Permeated against me by the DHS. How to get me out of the establishment was the focus of some management personnel. Even though they will not admit to what I am saying, but the records are there.

For the two years that I work there, never was I written out, nor did I ever receive a verbal or written warning. Only to be told one day that I neglected a resident. Lies! They wrote out their conspiracy statement against me and asked me to sign it. I said, "With all due respect, Ma', I am not signing this on grounds that it could incriminate me." So I refused to sign. As a matter of fact the very day that my evaluation was done and commended for good performance, it was the same day that I was terminated. Speaking of betraying someone with a kiss. Tell me about it because I'm living it. I saw it play out on me.

I sent the corporate an e-mail, telling them that I was wrongfully terminated. My e-mail was never addressed. I wanted to call Channel 6 News, but after talking things over with my wife, I decided to let go. Like I said earlier, that the character assassination against me, by the DHS, has caused me to lose friends. People that were willing to help us in the ministry, of course they will not admit to it just like how the management at the Forum also would not admit that these lies played a part in me losing my employment.

Another incident which I know very well that people will not admit to is when in the month of September 2011, my wife and I attended a fellowship meeting of the Ohio Baptist Bible Fellowship in Norwood, Ohio. To be exact, the meeting was held at 4255 Ashland Avenue, Norwood, Ohio 45212. When we arrived we were warmly received by the host pastor. I informed him that I would like to meet with the leadership of the fellowship, an opportunity I received. I believe the meeting was attended by the chairman, the state representative, and others. In that meeting, I appeal to the Body of Believes through the leadership for assistance for our congregation. They were well impressed and promised to take our request to the body in the business meeting.

By the time we were done with eating breakfast, before going in for the first section. I told my wife we will not receive the help we have asked for. "Why do you say that?" my wife asked. I told her something had just happened that changed everything. I then told of the overwhelming sentiment of awareness that came over me. In it I could hear a man telling the leaders, "You have to keep an eye on that guy, your black guest. He's not who he is pretending to be. As a matter of fact, the DHS is keeping a close eye on him."

When it came the time for the business meeting, rather the chairman speaking of our church as they did with other churches that went to the meeting requesting help, the chairman was speaking of us being a legal establishment. By the time the business meeting was over, I was being looked at more of a criminal. Then a fellow pastor, the chairman, pledged $100, which we still have yet have to receive. I also noticed that some of the pastors began to behave toward me, like that of the unbelievers. I felt so bad and humiliated. Upon my return from the Meeting, I told my pastor and mentors of all that took place. He apologized that I had to endure such. I don't discuss the spiritual side of me with him, reason being that I don't want him feeling somehow. Do I expect the chairman of the OBBF to admit that someone from the DHS spoke with him or spoke to someone who spoke with him? Of course not. So then what will cause the spreading of rumors, false accusations, and character assassination to stop? It will continue until there is a divine intervention.

To those of you who watch African movies, not only Africans movies, but movies in general, movies that has a message of real life events, when you watch them, just don't say "aman" (an expression of sympathy) when something bad is happening to an innocent person in the movies. But see it as a possibility that it could be you in real life. I don't watch much movies but for my present predicament, I will recommend that you watch the Christian movie called *The Price*. Perhaps it will help you understand my plight.

An image of the object suspended in midair behind my house.

# Copies of the Letters

Copy of the letter I wrote to the governor.

Emmett K. Shasha
4167 Arbury Ln
Columbus Ohio 43224

December 6, 2006

His Excellency
Honorable Ted Strickland
Governor Elect of the state Of Ohio

Dear Sir.
I salute and congratulate you on your recent election as governor of the state of Ohio. As your inauguration is anticipated let me say hats off to you. As you assume the leadership role as governor of this great state I strongly believe that there will be justices for the innocent. So that they can live in peace having a peace of mind.

Having ascended to such position of Authority there are so many important things letters, document etc. Coming across your deck of which my letter is one of the less expected. But in the name of human right and Justices I will highly appreciate if you will take a moment to read my letter and give it some consideration. For this I appeal to your Excellency to please give my letter your undivided attention.

I am Emmett K. Shasha, a peaceful law abiding resident of the City of Columbus Franklin County. A license minister of the gospel at the Columbus Baptist Temple. 5075 Cleveland ave, Columbus Ohio 43231. I AM NOT THE PASTOR.

I really done know how to commence expressing what I'm about to say, reason being that I'm to have no knowledge about it. You may think that I'm a lunatic but I'm not. It's for this reason that I'm writing to request your timely intervention. While I said you may think I'm a lunatic is that I done have a paper to show or give to back what I'm about to tell you. But with your position in authority you can get to know the true.

Your Excellency, there is no security organization or there affiliate in the city of Columbus who done know that I am a criminal even though in reality I have committed no crime. If the things I have writing to you in this letter be false let me be punish for it but if true let me live with a peace of mind.

I believe strongly that I am a victim of mistake and identity and this have caused me a lot of damage emotionally and character wise. I am being falsely accuse of crime I know nothing about because of this accusation I'm follow and monitor daily. I have no problem being follow or monitor it's the lies false rumens and gossip being spray about me that I done like.

Your Excellency, I done expect to meet with you because of your busy schedule but I will appreciate if you could have someone from your office to look in to the matter. Upon gartering your information I am willing to take a polygraph/lie dative test under the watchful eyes of your office representative. Its nearly four years since it all started.

Your Excellency, who knows maybe just maybe it's for matter such as these that you have come to power. While I await your responds May the LORD grant you wisdom.

Yours Truly,

Emmett K. Shasha

Copy of the letter that I wrote to the attorney general.

 **Sound Doctrine Baptist Fellowship International**
Rev. EMMETT K. SHASHA, PASTOR
5075 Cleveland Avenue. Columbus, Ohio 43231.(614)337-1801-(614)592-9598
Sdbrinternational0883@gmail.com
*"Fulfilling The Great Commission" Matthew, 28:19-20*

Date June 8, 2009

Richard Cordray
Attorney General Of Ohio
State Office Tower
30 E. Broad Street, 17th Floor
Columbus, Ohio 43215

Dear Sir.
    I am Rev. Emmett K. Shasha, Pastor of the above named church. I also work
for ResCare of central Ohio, 6170 Busch Blvd. Columbus, Ohio 43229 and for the
Emeritus; senior living at 690 cooper, Westerville, Ohio 43081.

Two and a half years ago I wrote the than Governor elected, His Excellency Ted
Strickland, now Governor. With the hope that he would have used his office to
look into situation that is affecting my character. I also sent a follow up e-mail to
his Excellency Office sometime this year reminding him of my letter. But up to
date I still have not heard a word from the Governor's Office.
I was watching Larry King live Wednesday night May 27, 2009. During which
time he interviewed a man, Mr. Jerry Lee Evans, who was wrongfully convicted;
causing him to spend 23 years of his life behind bars, for a crime he did not
commit. During the broad cast he also interviewed two other men, who had similar
fate as Mr. Evans.

I find it not only appalling; but very troubling. Reason being that I have the copy of
a research conducted by a group of men who also recorded the details of their
findings in a book 'Convicted But Innocent' according to their note. As a part of
their findings it was determined that the reason for most wrongful convictions
resulted from a "combination of errors. Eyes witness misidentification. Perjury by
a witness" etc.

One thing which stood out to me in this document is the case involving one Mr.
William Jackson, of Columbus. See attach.

Unless there is an intervention from your office or the office of the governor; I foresee that what happened to Mr. Jerry Lee Evans, Mr. William Jackson, and others, will likely happen to me. But I am trusting God through his son Jesus Christ that justice will take its full course, so that the innocent can live in peace with a peace of mind.

Sir, to retrospect; I was a member, now an affiliating member of the Columbus Baptist Temple. Located at 5075 Cleveland Ave. Columbus, Oh 43231. I was and still a peaceful law abiding resident of Columbus.

All was well until the fall of 2002, during the construction work of the Columbus Baptist Temple new building now occupied by parishioners. I was a volunteer on the project. I got to work one day and said thanks to the men that were working as I normally did every day. On this day there was a contractor, an elderly man laying bricks who said to me "go back to your country! We do not need you here; we do not want any foreigner here, go home."

I stood speechless. It was my first time seeing him, I did not know him. One of the men working on the project said to the bricks layer, chill! He is a volunteer from the church. The mason then said "I do not care let him go to his country".

We worked until the day was over, as I got back to work at the church the next day, the mason was there. Just as I started working, a black SUV driven by a black man drove up. The passenger in the front set a white man took my picture so I walk over to the SUV and asked why did you take my picture? The driver said to me you will see it in the newspaper.

It was not long I began to notice cars stalking me; I went to the police substation at the intersection of Morse and Karl road and reported it to the police on December 26, 2002. The officer doing the recording said that they were going to look into it. Sometime this year 2009 I went to the police substation to get a copy of the report, I was told to go down to the mean office. On April 5, 2009 I went to the Columbus Division of Police Record section to obtain a copy of the report only to be told that they had no such record. I received only a copy of a Telephone Harassment complains.

While no one (law enforcement personnel) has ever approached me on any issue; yet I suspected being accused as a thief, a murder, a Muslim and a Nigerian. All of which is false and baseless, gear toward destroying my reputation.

This attitude of false accusation and spreading of rumors is causing me harm. It is affecting the Ministry (Church) and my personal life.

I made two channel 4 NBC News appearances one was in 2003 and the other was made in 2005, they were done under the disguise of obtaining public sympathy for me. But the real reason I strongly believe these appearances were done with the hope that some would have identified me as being a criminal. Under this same pretend, I was interviewed by one of our program managers acting on the directive of the HR department of ResCare of central Ohio. Under this disguise; I was being interview for the company quarterly news letter mid 2008. Which still have yet to appear; even though since the interview about three or four news letter have come out.

Sometimes this year 2009 I spoke with the President of the Liberian Community in Columbus, Dr. LeRoy Z. Boikai, to see if he could use his office as President of the Community to help put a stop to the spreading of these rumors. I also gave him a paper of an observation that I made. See attach.
Sir. Upon your request I am available to come to your office at your convenience, to meet with you or any one whom you may destine to answer any question you might have with regard to my letter.
As I am being monitor from the air, on the ground and through my phone it's ok, all I am asking is that the false accusations against me and character assassination stop. I am appealing to your office to please look into my concern.
As I await a comprehensive respond from your office may the LORD grant you wisdom.
Thanks.

Respectfully Yours

Rev. Emmett K. Shasha

Cc: Copy Pre Pay Legal
Cc: Copy Dr. LeRoy Z. Boikai, President Liberian Community in Columbus.

ATTACHED
1. Letter to the governor elected.
2. Copy of an observation given to Dr. Boikai.
3. Copy of the reached mention.

Copy of the letter that I wrote to Maguire & Schneider L. L. P. (Pre-Paid Legal)

Rev. Emmett K. Shasha
4167 Arbury Lane
Columbus, Ohio 43224

MAGUIRE & SCHNEIDER L.L.P.
ATTORNEYS AT LAW
250 CIVIC CENTER DR. SUITE 500
COLUMBUS, OHIO 43215

June 8, 2009

Dear Sir/ Madam.
I am Rev. Emmett K. Shasha, Senior pastor of the Sound Doctrine Baptist
Fellowship International. Member ID# 10093846177.
I became a member of Pre Pay Legal because of a phrase in the third paragraph on
page seven of your hand book. It states "….simply ignore a problem and hope it
goes away" well! That exactly what I am face with; ignoring a problem and hoping
that it will go away. Or would have gone away.
I believe that I am a victim of mistake and identity. I suspect that I am being
stalking and accused of being a thief, a murder, a Muslim and a Nigerian.
Upon becoming a member of the Organization I spoke with one of your Attorneys
and fax him a copy of the letter I wrote the then Governor elected. He said that I
had a good case and then asked me for the case number; after I told him that I had
no such thing he said nothing really.
The false accusation and rumors spreading against me is harming the Ministry
(Church) where I serve as the senior Pastor. And my personal life. I do not know
how to go about it that is why I wrote the then Governor elected now Governor,
and that is why I am writing the Attorney general.
It is my hope that you will give my letter your undivided attention, and commence
legal proceeding to stop the destruction of my character.
Thanks.

Truly Yours

Rev. Emmett K. Shasha
M E M B E R

ATTACH
1. Letter to the Attorney General
2. Letter to the then Governor elected
3. Observation paper given to the Dr. L. Boikai, President of the Liberian Community in Columbus.
4. Copy of the research mention in the Attorney general letter

The reply to my letter from Pre-Paid legal.

**MAGUIRE & SCHNEIDER, L.L.P.** ATTORNEYS AT LAW
250 CIVIC CENTER DRIVE, SUITE 500    COLUMBUS, OHIO 43215   (614) 221-4479   FAX (614) 221-2033

*William C. Donahue*

January 19, 2011

Emmett K. Shasha
4167 Arbury Lane
Columbus, Ohio 43224-1704

| RE: | *Membership No.:* | *10093846177* |
|---|---|---|
| | *Intake No.:* | *515020* |
| | *Subject:* | *Letter to the Governor* |

Dear Mr. Shasha:

We have reviewed the information and documentation that you have provided in the above-referenced matter. Unfortunately, we have determined that there is no issue of law for us to address. Therefore, as attorneys, we are unable to offer any assistance or legal solution to your situation.

Thank you for using your Ohio Access to Justice/Pre-Paid Legal Services, Inc. membership.

We look forward to the opportunity to serve you in the future on other legal matters.

Very truly yours,

Maguire & Schneider, L.L.P.

William C. Donahue
Attorney at Law

WCD/lar

Copy of the letter I wrote to the president of the Liberian Community in Columbus.

Rev. Emmett K. Shasha
4167 Arbury Lane
Columbus, Ohio 43224


June 8, 2009

Dr. LeRoy Z. Boikai
President Liberian in Columbus, Inc
374 Howland Drive,
Gahanna, Ohio 43230


Dear Dr. Boikai.

Since I give you the paper of my observation the car in question has not return. But everything still remains the same. I wrote the Attorney General of Ohio a letter. I also attach a copy of the observation I give you to his letter.
I also wrote a letter to Pre Pay Legal sending them a copy of the attach to your letter, I mention in the Attorney General letter that a cc, copy of his letter was sent to you.
It is my hope that someone will look beyond the physical into the ram of the spiritual and come to term with the truth that an innocent man's life is being destroyed. Just as it was with Mr. Jerry Lee Evens, and others see Larry King Live 5/27/09 brow cast. I will keep you inform.

Truly Yours

Rev. Emmett K. shasha

Attach
  1. Letter to the Attorney General
  2. Letter to the then Governor elected
  3. Letter to Pre Pay Legal
  4. Observation paper I gave you
  5. Copy of the reached mention in the Attorney General Letter

Evidence that the letters sent were received.

**SENDER: COMPLETE THIS SECTION**

- Complete items 1, 2, and 3. Also complete item 4 if Restricted Delivery is desired.
- Print your name and address on the reverse so that we can return the card to you.
- Attach this card to the back of the mailpiece, or on the front if space permits.

**COMPLETE THIS SECTION ON DELIVERY**

A. Signature
X ☐ Agent ☐ Addressee

B. Received by (Printed Name) *Steve Atkinson* C. Date of Delivery

D. Is delivery address different from item 1? ☐ Yes
   If YES, enter delivery address below: ☐ No

JUN 11 2009

1. Article Addressed to:
HIS EXCELLENCY RICHARD CORDRAY
ATTORNEY GENERAL OF OH
STATE OFFICE TOWER
30 E. BROAD ST. 17TH FLOOR
COLUMBUS, OH 43215

3. Service Type
   ☐ Certified Mail ☐ Express Mail
   ☐ Registered ☐ Return Receipt for Merchandise
   ☐ Insured Mail ☐ C.O.D.

4. Restricted Delivery? (Extra Fee) ☐ Yes

2. Article Number
7009 0820 0000 5026 6902

PS Form 3811, February 2004     102595-02-M-1540

---

**SENDER: COMPLETE THIS SECTION**

- Complete items 1, 2, 3. Also complete item 4 if Restricted Delivery is desired.
- Print your name and address on the reverse so that we can return the card to you.
- Attach this card to the back of the mailpiece, or on the front if space permits.

**COMPLETE THIS SECTION ON DELIVERY**

A. Signature
X ☐ Agent ☐ Addressee

B. Received by (Printed Name) C. Date of Delivery

D. Is delivery address different from item 1? ☐ Yes
   If YES, enter delivery address below: ☐ No

1. Article Addressed to:
HON. Ted Strickland
P.O. BOX 1255
building
MINFORD OH
45643

3. Service Type
   ☒ Certified Mail ☐ Express Mail
   ☐ Registered ☐ Return Receipt for Merchandise
   ☐ Insured Mail ☐ C.O.D.

4. Restricted Delivery? (Extra Fee) ☐ Yes

2. Article Number
(Transfer from service label)
7005 2570 0000 2754 0178

PS Form 3811, February 2004   Domestic Return Receipt   102595-02-M-1540

```
              OAKLAND PARK PO
              COLUMBUS, Ohio
                 432249998
              3817950224 -0095
10/24/2011   (800)275-8777      10:50:46 AM

                 Sales Receipt
Product           Sale  Unit       Final
Description        Qty  Price      Price
                                   $18.30
WASHINGTON DC 20510
Zone-4 Express Mail
PO-Add Flat Rate Env
 3.10 oz.
Label #: EI165344215US
Tue 10/25/11 12:00 PM - Guaranteed
Delivery
Signature Requested
                                 ========
Issue PVI:                         $18.30

PVI Line Item Void                -$18.30
WASHINGTON DC 20510                 $18.30
Zone-4 Express Mail
PO-Add Flat Rate Env
 3.20 oz.
Label #: EI165344215US
Tue 10/25/11 12:00 PM - Guaranteed
Delivery
Signature Requested
                                 ========
Issue PVI:                         $18.30
                                 --------
Total:                             $18.30

Paid by:                           $18.30
VISA
                          XXXXXXXXXXXX254
  Approval #:           708918
  Transaction #:        440
  23 902990191

Order stamps at usps.com/shop or call
1-800-Stamp24.  Go to usps.com/clicknship
to print shipping labels with postage.
For other information call 1-800-ASK-USPS.
****************************************
Get your mail when and where you want it
with a secure Post Office Box. Sign up for
a box online at usps.com/poboxes
****************************************
****************************************

Bill#: 1000504496406
Clerk: 14

   All sales final on stamps and postage
   Refunds for guaranteed services only
        Thank you for your business
****************************************
****************************************
        HELP US SERVE YOU BETTER

   Go to: https://postalexperience.com/Pos

     TELL US ABOUT YOUR RECENT
         POSTAL EXPERIENCE

       YOUR OPINION COUNTS
****************************************
****************************************
```

Copy of the letter I wrote to the honorable senator.

 **Sound Doctrine Baptist Fellowship International**
**Rev. EMMETT K. SHASHA, PASTOR**
**5075 Cleveland Avenue. Columbus, Ohio 43231. (614)337-1801-(614)937-6602**
Sdbchurch07@yahoo.com
*"Fulfilling The Great Commission" Matthew. 28:19-20*

October 24, 2011

His Excellency
Honorable Rob Portman
United State Senator
338 Russell Senate Office Building
Washington, DC 20510

Dear Honorable Portman.

I am Rev. Emmett K. Shasha, senior pastor of the above name church. I also work for ResCare of Central Ohio, as a direct support staff, the head office is at 6170 Bush Blvd. Columbus, Ohio. I am also working at the Forum at Knightsbridge, located at 4625 Knightsbridge Blvd. Columbus Ohio, As an STNA.

A long awaited childhood dream for me was finally realize on the 18th of October, 2011 when I shook hands with two representatives from your office congratulating me after I took the oath of allegiance to the United States, thereby becoming a citizen of the United States.
As a boy growing up in my country of birth Liberia, all that was thought us was about America, to the point that many Liberians saw Liberia as the 51st States of the United States.
The fourteenth years of civil war that hit Liberia in 1989 displace many Liberians; I was blessed to come to the United States, ten years ago. After five years of living here and working two full time jobs, I was able to send for my wife and children. Today two of my children that are still at home with us, my wife and I have all become citizen of the United States. To God be the glory.

Your Honor. As a citizen of this great nation, I write to you first as a fellow American, I am also writing to you as my Senator, to acquaint you with the plight against my life. I have written to people in positions of authority, people who I know and believe that could be of some assistance to me, but up to the date of this letter nothing have been done, if anything, I believe things have gotten worse.

In December of 2006, I wrote the then Governor elect of Ohio His Honor. Ted Strickland, but I received no respond. In June of 2009 I wrote the Attorney General of Ohio Att. Richard Cordray, I received a phone called from a representative of his office who told me that the Attorney General of Ohio did not have jurisdiction over the area where I reside. (4167 Arbury Ln Columbus, OH 43224); that is like the United States Senator from Ohio telling me that he done represent Franklin County, even though Franklin County is in Ohio.

In June of 2009 I wrote the President of the Liberian Community in Columbus, in the person of Dr. Leroy Z. Boikai, last of all I wrote to Maguire and Schneider L. L. Attorneys of Prepay Legal, of which I am a member, I was told by them that they did not see the ground for a case. I believe it is because the pain I am going through is not been felt by them that why they responded in that way.

In 2003 Mandy Dryer of (NBC-4 TV New) did a story on me, which was follow by another one in 2005 when my family came to the States. It was done in the content of drawing public sympathy for the plight of my family that was still in Liberia. But the story behind the story was to put me on TV with the hope that someone will come forward to identify me; of what I will be telling you shortly.

In 2010 our Church was invited to be a part of a program held at the North YMCA, with the theme "We Are Family" with the many participations including the host, I am the only one who was feature in a four by three quarter by six and a half picture on the front of the 'This Week New' New Paper with few words.

Your Honor, as a citizen of this nation and a fellow Ohioan, I will appreciate highly if you would give mine complain your farthest attention.

I am a victim of mistake and identity, while it is true that no law enforcement officer have approach me on such matter, yet I have already been found guilty by the public for things I know nothing about. A Misrepresentation of my faith, A Misrepresentation of my Country of Birth and Character Assassination;

The false rumor being spread in this state and around the nation about me is harming me greatly. (Emotionally, physically and physiologically) this false rumor is also destroying the Ministry which I am pasturing. Many people that were a part of the church have left, Individual, Organization and Ministries whom we went to for help have all refuse to give us a helping hand.

In my place of work I am treated more like a criminal then a minister of the gospel. The false rumor and character assassination against me have destroyed my life.

I am being treated by the Department of Homeland Security, a committee on which you service as though I have committed some crime.

Your Honor. I have seen the lives of so many Americans destroyed, one time they said that they had no knowledge of the crime for which they were accused, yet they were found guilty and imprison some from five years to twenty six plus years. Did anyone believe them at the time no; yet after many years of false imperilment they were release with an apology. Am I the next victim? Only for the system to come back later when they realize the true to we are sorry? God forbid.

Your Honor. The accusation I am being accuse of is that I am a **Muslim, a Nigerian,** a **Thief,** and a **Murder.** All of which are lies. The drama being play out in my life is very similar to the story found in Genesis 39. God have called me to preach his word, all that I am asking you is to please intervene to save what is left of me and stop my name from dragging in the mud.

With your position on the committee, of Homeland Security, the truth and nothing but the whole truth can be known by you should you decided to act. I am available to meet with you at your office or a representative destine by you to answer any question you may have, even if it calls for a lie detective test.

While await your comprehensive responded. I beseech you; Honorable Senator, in the name of truth and justice to please employed the wisdom of God, as you conduct you own investigation to bring to light the true so that the rights of the innocent can be preserved
And that they may live in peace with a peace of mind. Please see attach for the letters mentions in this letter. Thanks.

Respectfully Yours


Rev. Emmett K. Shasha

Attach: Letter to Governor Ted Strickland
       Letter to Att. General Richard Cordray
       Letter to Dr. Leroy Z. Boika
       Letter to Maguire and Schneider L. L

Copy of the phone harassment report from the CDP.

## Columbus Division Of Police Preliminary Investigation

Case No. 08112183CPD
Report No. 08112183CPD.1
Report Date: 4/5/2008 6:52:38 AM

| | | | | |
|---|---|---|---|---|
| Subject | **552 - Telecommunication Harassment** | | | |
| Case Report Status | **Approved** | Date Entered | 4/5/2008 6:52:38 AM | Reporting Officer |
| Report Type | **Preliminary Investigation** | Entered By | Holt, Penny | Holt, Penny |
| Occurred On | **4/1/2008 8:00:00 AM** | Date Verified | 1/1/1900 | |
| (and Between) | **4/4/2008 8:00:00 AM** | Verified By | | |
| | | Date Approved | 4/5/2008 6:55:25 AM | |
| Location | **4167 Arbury Ln** | Approved By | **Holt, Penny** | Assisted By |
| Zip Code | **43224** | | | |
| Geo Code | | Connecting Cases | | |
| Zone | **Zone 1** | Disposition | **Active** | |
| Call Source | **TRU** | Clearance Reason | | |
| District | **706 District** | Date of Clearance | | |
| Vehicle Activity | | Reporting Agency | **Columbus Division Of Police** | |
| Vehicle Traveling | | Division | **Columbus Police** | |
| Cross Street | | Map | **Zone 1** | |
| Jurisdiction | **Columbus, OH** | | | |
| Means | | | | |
| Other Means | | | | |
| Motive | | | | |
| Other Motives | | | | |
| Threat Group | **No** | Incident Number | | |
| Latent Process | **Not Applicable** | Property Process | | |
| Location Of Dispatched Run | **4167 Arbury Ln** | Basic Called In | | |
| Tech Number | | Reporting Officer Assignment | | |
| Detective Notified | | Detective Name | | |
| Teletype # | | Unit Case File # | | |
| NIC # | | LEADS ID Number | | |

Report Narrative   R/P STATES THAT HE IS RECEIVING HANG UP CALLS.

## Offense Detail: 291721.90Z - Telecommunications Harassment

| | | | |
|---|---|---|---|
| Offense Description | 291721.90Z - Telecommunications Harassment | | |
| IBR Code | **90Z - All Other Offenses** | No. Prem. Entered | |
| IBR Group | **B** | Entry Method | |
| Crime Against | **SO** | Method of Entry For Motor Vehicle Theft | |
| ORC Code | **291721.90Z** | Method of Entry For Burglary/B&E | |
| Offense Completed? | **Yes** | Method of Entry For Burglary/B&E | |
| Larceny Type | | Direction of Entry | |
| Primary Location | **Single Family Home** | Secondary Location | |
| Hate/Bias | **No Bias/Not Applicable** | Force Level | |
| Domestic Violence | **No** | | |
| Method of Operation | | | |
| Using | | | |
| Criminal Activity | | | |
| Weapons/Force | | | |
| Type Security | | | |
| Tools Used | | | |
| Type Of Abuse | | Arrested By | |
| Warrant Filed By | | | |
| Offense Notes | | | |

| Entry/Exit Direction | Location | Type | Entry/Exit |
|---|---|---|---|
| | | | |

## Victim V1: SHASHA, EMMETT

| | | | |
|---|---|---|---|
| Victim Code | **V1** | Victim Of | |
| Victim Type | | | |
| Name | **SHASHA, EMMETT** | DOB | Place of Birth |

# Columbus Division Of Police Preliminary Investigation

Case No. 08112183CPD
Report No. 08112183CPD.1
Report Date: 4/5/2008 6:52:38 AM

Columbus Division Of Police
120 Marconi Blvd
Columbus, OH 43215
614 645-4545

**2**

| | | | | | | |
|---|---|---|---|---|---|---|
| AKA | | Age | 46 | | SSN | |
| Alert(s) | | Sex | Male | | DLN | |
| | | Race | Black | | DLN State | |
| Address | 4167 Arbury Ln | Ethnicity | Not of Hispanic Origin | | DLN Country | |
| CSZ | Columbus, OH 43224 | Ht. | | | Occupation/Grade | |
| | | Wt. | | | Employer/School | |
| Home Phone | 337-1801 | Eye Color | | | Res. County | |
| Work Phone | | Hair Color | | | Res. Country | |
| E-mail | | Facial Hair | | | Resident Status | Resident |
| Attire | | Complexion | | | Testify | |
| Injury | | | | | Will Prosecute | |
| Circumstances | | | | | | |

| Law Enforcement Officer Killed or Assaulted Information | Type | | Justifiable Homicide Circumstances | |
|---|---|---|---|---|
| | Assignment | | | |
| | Activity | | | |
| | Other ORI | | | |

Victim Taken To — Transported By
Treated/Pronounced By — Ordered in
Ordered In Date/Time — Can ID
Victim Relationship to Suspect — Has lived as spouse within one year of alleged incident
Person related by blood or marriage with offender — The other 'Natural' parent of the offender's child
Victim Currently live with the offender — Has victim resided with the offender in the past

Victim Injury/Severity
Injury Type — Injury Severity — Injury Location

Injuries Visible — Victim called police
Reporting Officer Assignment — Reporting Officer Assignment
Victim Actions — Was suspect at the scene when officer arrived Jurisdiction
Is there an existing CPD/TPO against offender Case Number — Had the suspect been drinking or using drugs If yes, Location
Will Victim be Staying at temporary address? Confidential — Were children present at the scene?
Has the victim been drinking or using drugs

Children Present
Age — Sex — Interviewed

Is victim a juvenile? — Has FCCS been notified?
Primary Aggressor — Order to Prosecutor Office

Victim Offender Relationships
Offender — Relationship

Victim Notes

My 6 × 6 picture in the front page of the This WeekNews News
Paper, January 28, 2010, edition.

## 'WE ARE FAMILY...'

By Ann Tormet/ ThisWeek

Originally from Liberia, Emmett Shasha of the Northland area chats about the African country with Christine Look and her 7-year-old daughter, Zoe, at the "We are Family ... Yesterday, Today & Tomorrow" event. The North YMCA on Sandalwood Place sponsored the multicultural event Sunday, Jan. 24. People originally from Korea, Somalia, Ghana, Italy, Germany, Liberia and other countries were at the event to talk about their cultures. The event also offered salsa dance lessons, display booths and

Copy of my observation, which was sent to the attorney general.

### Observation

On this date (01/26/09) I got to work at about 2:40 pm after dropping my wife to work. I open the trunk of my car and began to change the left tail light bulb; at about 2:50 pm this car show's up and park near the dump stock, a no parking area. The plate No: (ENE 8054). This is about the third time. The first time this car shows up, I had dropped my wife to work. I got to work thirty mines earlier, I lay the car set back to take a nap while waiting for time when I got out of the car to go in the building there was this same car. I suspect on his second visit he used his camera phone to take my picture, but I said nothing as I walk by. Emmett.

Date 01/27/09 I got to work today at about 2:52pm after dropping my wife to work. The very same car with plate NO:( ENE 8054) was park in the same place as the day before. As I walk by I again notice him with his phone, it appear to me that he was recording as I walk to enter the building. I clock in and made my rounds and came back out in twenty mines the car was gone. Emmett

Let me state here that one thing that did happen was that a few days after the receipt of my letter by the then attorney general, the car in my observation did stop coming, not because they had stop stalking me, but because for him, his cover was opened. I could state the plates of many others, but it will do me no good. Besides, the only reason I mentioned him was because he was one of the overzealous ones.

I know very well that there will be a mixed reaction once people commence the reading of this book. Having read it thus far some might begin to think, "Are there people who really get these kinds of awareness that are mention here?"

I would not have written this book if the monitoring of my life in this country has stopped. People would normally write a book after they have had an experience, but it is not so in my case. I am writing while going through these experiences. I did not sit down to do a research of materials before writing, the reason being that I am the research; the things are happening to me. I indeed will include some research notes with quotations to let the public know that I am not the first to have had my name dragged in the mud. Oftentimes people will say, "Big brother watching." Who is the big brother that is watching and from what stands, that is which branch of the system? They can't say. Well, in my case that big brother is the DHS. And the information that is out there about me that has caused people to know more about me than I myself are all false, the once being carry around by the DHS.

That is the reason why I will include some research notes: so that you can see others whose lives were destroyed by the system. Perhaps it will help to open your eyes to realize and let you know that you are only blessed not to be accused falsely. But that doesn't mean that you are immune from it. It could happen to you at any given moment.

Remember the words of my old army friend that was mentioned earlier? "They can do it to anybody and there's nothing you can do about it." Seen what was happening to me I became very curious to know if I was the first or if I was the only one. Well, I am not the first to be accused falsely but the first to know beforehand of what they are or were about to do before they did it.

Having gotten to know that I am not the first, I then decided to do a research, and what I found out was appalling. While I will be proving the names of those whose work I will be quoting from, I will only use the initials of people whose story I will mention, because I do not have their permission to use their names. I think that it is good for the general public to be aware of what their elected officials and their appointees are doing to the innocent in the name of security and turning a blind eye to justice.

I feel compelled to mention this story; I will also include a picture of this story. Perhaps it will also help you to see clearly into the plight I am undergoing. Normally, if a newspaper features you on its front page in 4 & a equator by 6 & a half inches photo, it means that there is a lot to be said about you that made it to the front page. It is expected that such a story will cover about ten, fifteen to even twenty paragraphs, but not a four-line sentence paragraph.

This Week Community Newspaper, January 28, 2010 edition, front page with no story, I say no story because the few lines paragraph did not worth a 4 & a equator by 6 and a half inches picture of me; looking beyond the few lines of sentence to see the bigger picture for which this picture of me was place on front page in the first place, became my concerned.

I was invited to the North YMCA, on Sandalwood Place to participate in a program: "We Are Family . . ." which is seen no where here in the photo. Of the many counties mentioned in the journalist's note, none of their representatives was seen anywhere in the picture. None of the organizers of the program made the photo list. Do you see something wrong here?

In life, I have been blessed to have attended one or more occasions. While the TV news or the newspapers will speak of the invited guests, those who organized the program are the ones featured in the photo lineup. It's like being invited to a wedding ceremony without the photo of the people that are making the day. You featured someone who was just invited to eat. Isn't it a bit unreal? Except there was a motive.

The woman talking with me, I believe, was a co-worker of the woman who took the picture of me that made the front page story.

# 'WE ARE FAMILY...'

By Ann Tormet/*ThisWeek*

Originally from Liberia, Emmett Shasha of the Northland area chats about the African country with Christine Look and her 7-year-old daughter, Zoe, at the "We are Family ... Yesterday, Today & Tomorrow" event. The North YMCA on Sandalwood Place sponsored the multicultural event Sunday, Jan. 24. People originally from Korea, Somalia, Ghana, Italy, Germany, Liberia and other countries were at the event to talk about their cultures. The event also offered salsa dance lessons, display booths and

The objective of Ann Tormet of the 'This Week' was to put me on display, just like the flocks from Channel 4 NBC News, with the hope that someone will come forth to identify me as an evildoer. The funny thing is that after my Channel 4 NBC News appearance and the feature in the 'This Week Community Newspaper', our church was having a very important program to which I invited both the journalist from the newspaper and the channel 4 newscaster via mail. None of them responded nor did they turn up.

The observance of our church's anniversary was not new wealthy, or maybe that was the last thing they were expecting to see since in fact, the man inviting them is supposed to be evil and should be thrown behind bars. Receiving and honoring an invitation from him was the last thing on their mind.

Copy of the invitation letters to Ann Tormet of the "This Week" newspaper.

 **Sound Doctrine Baptist Fellowship International**
### Rev. EMMETT K. SHASHA, PASTOR
**5075 Cleveland Avenue. Columbus, Ohio 43231. (614)337-1801-(614)592-9598**
Sdbfinternational0883@gmail.com
*"Fulfilling The Great Commission" Matthew. 28:19-20*

February 21, 2010

Miss. Ann Tormet
This Week Community News Papers
7801 N. Central Dr.
Lewis Center, OH 43035


Dear Miss Ann Tormet.

Greetings in the name of our Lord and soon coming King, Jesus Christ; in commemoration of the SOUND DOCTRINE BAPTIST FELLOWSHIP INT; Second anniversary celebration, we the saints of the above church, in collaboration with the COLUMBUS BAPTIST TEMPLE wish to invite you and your entire family, friends and co-workers to grace this occasion.

The message will be brought forth by Pastor Paul M. Gabriel, of the COLUMBUS BAPTIST TEMPLE. Come and be blessed and be a blessing. The service will take place at the above address.

Activities are as follows:

Friday, April 2, 2010 Revival Service @ 6:00 PM
Sunday, April 4, 2010 Divine Worship Service @ 2:30 PM


During the divine Worship Service a SPECIAL OFFERING will be raised for the Church Building Project. There will be a dinner after the service.

Yours In the Lord's Vineyard,

Bro. Aaron Armah
Acting Church Secretary

Approved: Rev. Emmett K. Shasha
Senior Pastor

The letter to Mandy Dryer of Channel 4TV news.

 **Sound Doctrine Baptist Fellowship International**
### Rev. EMMETT K. SHASHA, PASTOR
**5075 Cleveland Avenue. Columbus, Ohio 43231. (614)337-1801-(614)592-9598**
Sdbfinternational0883@gmail.com
*"Fulfilling The Great Commission" Matthew. 28:19-20*

**February 21, 2010**

Miss. Mandy Dryer
NBE4
Dublin, Ohio 43016

Dear Miss Dryer.

Greetings in the name of our Lord and soon coming King, Jesus Christ; in commemoration of the SOUND DOCTRINE BAPTIST FELLOWSHIP INT; Second anniversary celebration, we the saints of the above church, in collaboration with the COLUMBUS BAPTIST TEMPLE wish to invite you and your entire family, friends and co-workers to grace this occasion.

The message will be brought forth by Pastor Paul M. Gabriel, of the COLUMBUS BAPTIST TEMPLE. Come and be blessed and be a blessing. The service will take place at the above address.

Activities are as follows:

Friday, April 2, 2010 Revival Service @ 6:00 PM

Sunday, April 4, 2010 Divine Worship Service @ 2:30 PM

During the divine Worship Service a SPECIAL OFFERING will be raised for the Church Building Project. There will be a dinner after the service.

Yours In the Lord's Vineyard,

Bro. Aaron Armah
Acting Church Secretary

Approved: Rev. Emmett K. Shasha
Senior Pastor

# RESEARCH FINDINGS

Having mentioned the newspaper story, let's get back to seeing some discovery that were found while researching to see if I was the only victim of character assassination.

With the heading "10,000 Innocent People Convicted Each Year, Study Estimates . . . ," C. Ronald Huff of the Ohio State University made the staggering discovery from a research survey conducted by him and other researchers of people that were wrongfully convicted.

"Columbus, Ohio. About 10,000 people in the United States may be wrongfully convicted of serious crimes each year, a new study suggests.

The results are based on a survey of 188 judges, prosecuting attorneys, public defenders, sheriffs, and police."

He made an important observation why were there so many wrongful convictions. "The study also found that most important factor leading to wrongful conviction is eyewitness misidentification." Doing the survey, he asked respondents to estimate the prevalence of wrongful convictions in the United States. The response was phenomenal to the shame of a civilized world.

"About 72 percent estimated that less than 1 percent—but more than zero—of conviction were of innocent people." "Based on these results, he estimated conservatively that 0.5 percent of 1,993.880 convictions for index crimes in 1990 were of innocent people. (Index crimes, which are reported by the FBI, are murder and non-negligent manslaughter, forcible rape, aggravated assault, robbery, burglary, larceny-theft, motor vehicle theft, and arson.) That would result in an estimated 9,969 wrongful conviction."

In the research, he cites the case of a Columbus man who spent five years behind bars. "William Jackson, a Columbus man, spent five years behind bars in the early 1980s. For rapes later determined to have been committed by a physician who was similar in appearance and had the same last name".

Does this statement sound familiar? If you can recall, I mentioned how that one day when my pastor and mentor was through preaching, and just as he exited the pulpit, I mounted it saying that I am a victim of mistaken identity, and that people were stalking me. After making the statement, I also mentioned walking outside. Meanwhile, a man in the church who had been revealed to me in the spirit realm as being one of those that had his eyes on me followed me outside. He asked me whether I knew a man whose name he called. When I said no, he then asked me, "Are you not a Nigerian?" I said "No, I am a Liberian." He then said to me, "All of you look alike." To which I said, "No, I look like myself."

Putting one and one together, one will realize that I am highly suspected of being a Nigerian. There had been times when people were throwing hints at me will say, "Oh, you're a Nigerian, right?" Or they will greet me in a Muslim way of greeting, knowing for sure that I am a Christian but refusing to recognize me as such. Or they will say something like, "You want to kill me too." No offense to the peaceful, law-abiding Nigerian, but let me reiterate that I am a born Liberian.

The funny thing about it is that some of these people who knew me all along to be a Christian and a Liberian, after they have encounter the lies being spread about me have, all of a sudden, behaved somewhat differently toward me.

When I became a member of the Columbus Baptist Temple, I met a practical black lady in the church whom I also believe was a member. I met her there in 2001. We greeted each other every time. Never did she tell me of her husband being a Muslim until the lies of me being a Muslim started spreading. It was then that she came to me and said, "Oh, you know my husband is a Muslim." I was like, "What do you want?" "Oh, just for us to pray for him." Mind you, this was in 2003. From 2001, she knew that I was a member of the caring partners. Never did she ask me or any member of the caring partners for prayers concerning her husband.

They will say something like "Did you say that you were a Christian or Muslim?" Or, "We thought that you were from Nigeria and a Muslim." I was like, "We? You and who make up the 'we'?" And then they would say, "Oh, what I mean is that I thought you were a Nigerian and a Muslim."

As for the ones that are perpetuating the character assassination against me, they and their collaborators called me anything but a Christian, which I am. As my character is being distorted, dehumanized, and defamed by the DHS, as my name continue to be dragged in the mud, the only thing that has and is keeping my head above water is the assurance and courage that I get from the Holy Bible, which is the word of God. It's like what David said in the psalm, *"Save me, O God; for the waters are come in unto my soul. I sink in deep mire, where there is no standing: I am come into deep waters, where the floors overflow me. I am weary of my crying: my throat is dried: mine eyes fail while I wait for my God. They that hate me without a cause are more than the hairs of mine head: they that would destroy me, being mine enemies wrongful, are mighty: than I restored that which I took not away"* (Psalms 69:1-4).

The admonishment from James and Peter's letters in James 1:2-4: *"My brethren, count it all joy when ye fall into divers temptation; Knowing this, that the trying of your faith worketh patience. But let patience have her perfect work, that ye may be perfect and entire, wanting nothing."*

And 1 Peter 2:12: *"Having your conversation honest among the Gentiles; that, whereas they speak against you as evildoers, they may by your good works, which they shall behold, glorify God in the day of visitation."*

The quotation continues: "No one has ever known for sure how many women Dr. Jackson raped while the wrong man was in prison. He had five more years to continue his serial rape."

Huff and his fellow researchers "found that most wrongful conviction resulted from a combination of errors. The main cause in more than half of the cases—52.3 percent—was eyewitness misidentification." As stated earlier, it's like what I said then and continue to say, which of course no one wants to believe. I am a victim of mistakes identity.

Huff continues to say in his findings that "the next most common main cause was perjury by a witness, which contributed to 11 percent of the convictions. Other problems included negligence by criminal justice officials, coerced confessions, frame ups by guilty parties, and general overzealousness by officers and prosecutors" (These Quotations are from: researchnews.osu.edu/archive/ronhuff.htm [12/1/2008]).

The quotes from these researches will explain why I am being treated in this way. What do you mean? one may ask.

In June of 2006, that was about six years ago, when I wrote the then governor elect of the state of Ohio to inform him of my plight, I even urged His Excellency with a word of wisdom saying, "Who knows, maybe, just maybe, it's for matter such as these that you have come to power." I believe my plead landed on deaf ears, of the attorney general and the honorable senator. I told all of these officials of the government that I was and is willing to take a polygraph exam to prove my innocence. But the fact that they have all concluded in their mind that I am guilty as alleged, they thought it insignificant to reply to my letters.

Rather than responding, I believe they muster every apparatus necessary to their disposal to prove their point: that I am guilty. That is the reason for which they have all refused to act in the interest of justice and human rights. After all, who is that African to come out and say that the DHS is tarnishing his reputation. To further enhance the research, I'm including quotes from the Fact Sheet of the Innocence Project on Post Conviction DNA Exonerations before the quotation let me mention here that the most time that the DHS increases its network around me is when holidays are approaching and if I go out to attend an event. On other day, they will tend to relax a bit while keeping a watch. Some of you reading this book have friends that are a part of what I am saying. Pick up your phone and give them a call. If they want to be truthful, they will tell you exactly what I am saying.

"DNA exoneration cases have provided irrefutable proof that wrongful conviction are not isolated or rare events, but arise from systemic defects that can be precisely identified and addressed; For more than 15 years, the innocence project has work to pin point these trend."

According to the Fact Sheet of the Innocence Project. Like other researchers, here again eyewitnesses plays a road of misidentification.

"Eyewitness Misidentification Testimony was a factor in 72 percent of post-conviction DNA exoneration cases in the US make it the leading cause of these wrongful convictions. At least 40 percent of these eyewitness identification involved a cross racial identification (race data is currently only available on the victim, not for non-victim eyewitness). Studies have shown that people are less able to recognize faces of a different race than their own."

Remember the saying of the man who I said followed me out from the church after I made the statement that I was the victim of mistaken identity, how he had asked me for a man, and if I was a Nigerian. And when I said no, he replied "All of you look alike." This here confirms the racial discrimination issue.

> False confessions and incriminating statements lead to wrongful conviction in approximately 27 percent of cases. 28 of DNA exonerees pled guilty to crimes they did not commit. The Innocence Project encourages police department to electronically record all custodial interrogation in their entirety in order to prevent coercion and to provide an accurate record of the proceedings.
>
> Informants contributed to wrongful convictions in 18 percent of cases. When informant testimony is used, the Innocence Project recommends that judge instruct the jury that most informant testimony is unreliable it may be offered in return for deals, special treatment, or the dropping of charges. (The Innocence Project.org/content/Facts)

I will mention a few more stories, after which, I will conclude this book with an appeal to the honorable United States Congress as a United States citizen to please use the resources at their disposal to conduct an investigation of all that I have written in this book. I say unto you, honorable members of Congress, as a peaceful, law-abiding citizen, that I am available at your most convenient time to meet with any committee to conduct a lie test/polygraph exam to prove my innocence.

I said at the start of this book that no law enforcement personnel had ever talked to me concerning all that I have mentioned of myself in this book, yet I have been found to be guilty by the DHS and the public that have accepted these lies that are being perpetrated against me. I am only now awaiting sentencing according to public opinion. A quote from Presumed-Guilty-Innocent-Wrongly-Convicted/dp/0879756438:

The American judicial system is far too often a source of injustice for the innocent rather than justice for the guilty. Despite all the alleged protections built into the trial process, a person facing criminal charges is virtually presumed guilty until proven innocent—not the reverse . . . innocent American who each year are convicted of serious crimes they did not commit. Many are convicted of crimes that did not even occur.

PB&BRD Plead guilty to a 1979 Mississippi rape and murder they didn't commit. After the two men were threatened with death penalty, they testified against a third innocent defendant, LR, and received life sentences. DNA testing obtained by Innocence project New Orleans led to the three men's exonerations in 2010.

LB served three years in Florida prison after pleading guilty to a rape he did not commit. He has said he was threatened with a life sentence and coerced to plead guilty by the prosecutor and his court-appointed attorney. (innocenceproject.org)

I know that the DHS has, within its ranks, some very decent people. On the other hand, there are those who are there who believe in the "more days more dollars," and whatever they can do to keep a paycheck coming, that they will do.

We all saw and heard the scary tracks of imminent danger employed by some to get our nation into a senseless war. The "wolf cry," which resulted in thousands of the precious resources of this nation: the lives of our young men and women, being lost and billions of dollar spent. Rather than destroying the lives of innocent people by accusing them falsely and doing everything possible to make it appear real, they should learn and imitate the example of the former Illinois governor. Why should it always have to be the little ones to see the nakedness of the emperor? (Proverb indicating that something is wrong with the system.)

For those of you that will read this book and maybe think to yourself, it is not possible for someone to know the things that are being said in this book without someone saying something to the writer of this book. Well, remember that I mentioned earlier that there are two realms at work here: both the spiritual and the physical realms. There are those who think and believe that the physical is all to it. You too maybe thinking that way, but the physical earth you now see came from things that you don't see. The more real of these two is the spiritual, and it is the spiritual that determines what goes on in the physical realm. Don't take my word for it; read it for yourselves from the Old Testament's book of Job. Also read this verse; it might help open your eyes: Acts 2:17, *"I will pour out of my Spirit upon all flesh: and your sons and your daughters shall prophesy, and your young men shall see visions, and your men shall dream dreams."*

If you want to know what will come to pass in the physical, all you have to do is go to the spiritual to find out. Some of you reading this book have friends that work at the college and other monitoring agency. Ask them just how many times, when I am working in my backyard or sitting in my office in the basement, that I write on a paper and put it out for them to read in response to something they said.

Why do I do it? Because as they are monitoring me they are able to see a dime lying on the ground, just as they are able to read the sub headline of a news paper by putting out a quick respond to what they are saying will let them know that I really don't need someone physically to tell me what you are doing to me, once it concerned me I will know it. I boast not, but to God be the glory. "Since 1973, over 130 people have been released from death rows throughout the country due to evidence of their wrongful convictions. In 2003 alone, 10 wrongfully convicted defendants were released from death row.

"I cannot support a system which, in its administration, has proven so fraught with error and has come so close to the ultimate nightmare, the state's taking of innocent life . . . Until I can be sure that everyone sentenced to death in Illinois is truly guilty, until I can be sure with moral certainty that no innocent man or woman is facing a lethal injection, no one will meet that fate" (Governor George Ryan of Illinois, January 2000, in declaring a moratorium on execution in his state, after the thirteenth Illinois death row inmate had been released from prison due to wrongful conviction. In the same time period, twelve others had been executed.)

Reading the governor's quotes, he made mention of "ultimate nightmare." Who could better explain nightmare other then the players themselves? Under the heading 'The Wrongful Conviction a Way of Life' published May 26, 2011, and posted by Jeffrey Rosen quoting a judge, "The ghost of the innocent man convicted," "unreal dream," "convicting the innocent."

> Brandon L. Garrett shows that it can be a nightmarish reality." "Since the late 1980s, DNA testing has exonerated more than 250 wrongly convicted people, who spent an average of 13 years in prison for crimes they didn't commit.

> Almost 90 percent of the 250 innocent people later exonerated were falsely convicted of rape, or rape and murder, and 40 of the actually confessed to crimes they didn't commit, most adding specific details that only the real culprit could have known. How did this happen?

> Garrett describes how the police, intentionally or not, fed details of the crime to the suspects—and then recorded only portions of the interrogations so that it was difficult for defense lawyers and jurors to

reconstruct the truth. Even the selectively recorded interrogations make for painful reading, as the suspects offer facts that are inconsistent with what happened, and the police browbeat them into false confessions.

While we appreciate the system, there is a need for an overhauling, something we will leave to the professional to give their recommendations. In continuing to show how I am being affected by the system under the umbrella of the DHS, I will employ more quotations.

In addition to false confession, eyewitness wrongly identified the accused in 76 percent of the 250 cases. The unreliability of witness identifications is now widely known, but Garrett was surprised to discover how flagrantly unreliable the procedures were in the cases he examined. In 78 percent of the trials, he found evidence that police contaminated the eyewitness identifications with suggestive methods, like indicating which suspect in a lineup should be selected, or conducting lineups where one suspect obviously stood out from the others.

Of those exonerated by DNA, 70 percent were from minorities, and nearly half of the rape cases involving blacks or Hispanics, the victims were white. Where were the courts in all of these 250 miscarriages of justice? In 10 percent of the cases, appellate courts called the evidence of the innocent people's guilt "overwhelming." (www.nytimes.com/2011/05/29/books/review/book-review-conviciting-the-innocent)

In an Editorial Reviews from the Library Journal: "Most persons who are arrested are de facto guilty of something. This presumption of guilt, when it replaces the de jure presumption of innocence, leads to wrongful convictions. Yant, commentary editor of the Columbus Dispatch, clearly has the evidence to prove this thesis as he collects several dozen examples of justice gone awry . . . Yant uses a journalistic style to show how police and prosecutors, whether acting in good faith or not, sometime abuse their power" (John Broderick, Stonehill Coll., North Easton, Mass. Copyright 1991 Reed Business Information, Inc.)

"Normal everyday people think this doesn't happen but it does. People don't want to believe that prosecutor, sheriffs, or judges that they vote into office could or would deliberately convict the wrong man or woman. It happens every day and people don't care. Why? If it were an animal wrongly accused of biting someone, and put to death, people would be outraged, but when it is a person, it is like, "So what?" (Amazon.com/Presumed-Guilty-Innocent-Wrongly-Convicted/dp/0879756438)

I could go on citing more and more instances by giving one quotation after another of people whose lives were destroyed by the very system they have come to know to be the very best in the world. Like I said earlier, these people did not see any of these thing coming, but when it did come upon them, they try to plead their innocence. It is sad to know that the system that should had been there to protect them was the very one that were pushing a guilty penalty on them.

As you read in the quotes, some of these people were threatened by the very people who they cast their vote for. Others were simply ignored. If these things were not happening to me, I will have no need to say them. The shoe is on my foot and I am feeling the pain (a proverb of distress).

The book of James says, *"Let no man say when he is tempted, I am tempted of God: for God cannot be tempted with evil, neither tempteth he any man: But every man is tempted, when he is drawn away of his own lust, and enticed. Then when lust hath conceived, it bringeth forth sin: and sin, when it is finished, bringeth forth death. Do not err, my beloved brethren"* (Holy Bible, KJV)

I wrote this quotation from the book of James to tell of what took place in 2009. How true are these words, *"Do not err, my beloved brethren."* I mentioned earlier how a man came to my aunt's shop while I was serving as the manager. He was sent to kill me by means of a spiritual incantation, which he had pre-interwoven himself with a spell before coming to see me so that if I refuse to give him what he asked of me, that upon leaving my presence, I should immediately get sick and die.

In that way, no one will know what happened, and no one will be blamed. Well, it would have succeeded had the voice not spoken to me from my heart, warning me to give him anything he asked of me.

I can say that similar thing took place back in 2009, as a result of what the DHS is doing to me. The DHS, as an entity, did not order it, but someone who worked with the department somehow spoke with someone. This is what took place: the person that worked with the DHS was friendly with someone who was a spiritualist. On many occasions, they went to consult this spiritualist before going out, to find out what their day would be like. During one of the said visits, the person told the spiritualist about me.

"We listen to this guy every day and all he talks about is spiritual things, but he's a bad guy, and we are trying to apprehend him. But it still proving hard for us." At that, the spiritualist said, "We can get him without touching him." "Is that possible?" the person from DHS asked. "Yes," the spiritualist replied. And added, "Give me his name and address."

The spiritualist then proceeded to interweave the incantation on a letter addressed to me. The messenger in the white envelope with no return address was a snake about seven to ten incense in length. It was brown in color with white belly. Upon receiving the letter, once I opened it the invisible snake will leap on me and bite me. I will feel the pain and see the blood and the wound physically, but I will not know what caused it.

As soon as my blood makes contact with the floor or with the ground, that would have been the end of me. That was the plan. Well! It's like I said, that I asked the Lord for protection and revelation and he granted me both. The day I picked up my mail that contained the enchanted messenger, I sat at the dinner room table to open and read my mails. When I got to this mail, the voice of the Lord did not speak to me as it did in the past, but an overwhelming sentiment of danger came over me. I did not open the letter but put it aside and picked up another letter to open until I went through all.

At last I again picked up the letter to open. As I attempted again, the sentiment of danger came over me. I did not open it but took it outside and folded it in my hand and threw it in the trash. I did not go to the Lord in prayer to ask him to reveal to me what it was. But in a vision that night, I saw myself throwing the letter away after crushing it in my hand. Just as it hit the trash container, the snake came out, running away from me. Then the revelation of what took place was shown to me as you have just read. The DHS did not tell this spiritualist to do what he did, but a person who works for the department has contact with this spiritualist who was doing their friend a favor to eliminate me spiritually.

The shame of this de-characterization of my integrity has taken its toll on me, my family, and the church. It is in this light that I am appealing to the honorable members of the United States Congress, in this public manner to please take a look in to my complaint.

As you read this book, I urge you to remove Emmett from the picture. Instead put your own name, the names of your grandparents (for I am a grandparent), put the name of your father (for I am a father), put the name of your husband (for I am a loving husband), or anyone of your relatives. I am that to my family.

Once you have done that, ask yourselves this question: "What will I do if it were one of my relatives that is so dear to me? What will I do?"

To the United State Congress, I am not asking you, honorable people, for sympathy, nor am I asking for empathy. I am appealing to you in the name of justice and human right. I am appealing to you through this medium for your intervention so that the innocent can live in peace, and have a peace of mind. It is my honest prayer that my integrity that is being destroyed by the DHS will be saved as provided for by the constitution of the land and encoded in the Declaration of Independence.

Do not say, "Oh whatever!" for you could be the next; in short, "it can happen to you."

No offense to the dozens of white people out there. I love you with the loved of Christ, but I just have to say that it was a white man, a mason, that started it all. In protest of what the DHS is doing to me for almost two years, I placed a sticker on my cars that read, "What will you do, when you realize that you have accused me falsely?"

# THE BROAD AUDIENCES

The broad audiences that will be reading this book will comprise of nobles and commoner, professional, scholars, and simplistic individuals, as well those that are articulate; Of all the would be readers the once that will be prick at hearts will be those of a professional unit that is those of the security establishment; why do I say that, a section from the book says **"when foolishness overpower wisdom . . . but that of men with the motive of greed"**

As this particular group of professionals read the book some of them will employ wisdom, in comprehending and digesting the message there in contained; the imprudence once whose objective is greed will be out for avenged against the author. **'Avenged against the author!'** pretty strong words some will say; 'Yep in deed', 'this is a free country which condone the freedom of speech, the freedom of press etc'. Yes! But to what entrant?

I will here give a scenario and let you decide; about a year or so a resident alien recorded a police brutality during an arrest; that resident alien than forwarded the recording to CNN, which also broadcasted it in its news broadcasting, few days after the airing of the story, it was then determent by law enforcements that this resident alien green cars had expire. Was it for notoriety that this resident alien submitted the police course of action to the news organization? I guess not, seeking justice for the one that was being arrested, I strongly believe was his motive. I believe he knew that his green card had expire but as a human who having to be in the right place at the right time what was he to do?

Let's argue it for argument sack: because his green card had expires, he sees a car about to run over a child, and from his vantage point he is able to rescue the child, to prevent the child from being run over. What should he do? Would he had been hail as a hero for saving the child's life? I believe so; would anyone have known of the expiration of his green card? Most likely not, but when it came to exposing the ills of the society it was not in their favor therefore the whole world got to know of the expiration of his green card.

When did they really get to know that his green card had expire was it before or after the jungle justice. Would anyone have known the truth apart from his recording certainly not. Remember the story of RK?

"But it was the way that he almost died, in a severe beating by Los Angeles police officers, that made him a reluctant symbol of police brutality and spurred a conversation

111

about race, economics and justice in America. The subsequent riot a year later, after the acquittal and mistrial of the four officers charged in the beating, was the "nation's deadliest urban race riot since the Civil War," according to Lou Cannon in his book "Official Negligence." If there was no recording who would have known the truth?

Posted by Alicia W. Stewart. CNN.com Identity editor.

Someone once said that **"All it takes for evil to prevail is for good men to do nothing"**
It is not only in law enforcement that you find those good men; at most they are the ones that show concern for the cause of human right and justice.

In the confines of the law; sometimes those that are expected to uphold the law they are the very once that breaks it with impunity, yet they claim that they were only doing their job, hats off to them. I suppose you will read or have read in the quotations of what the authority sometimes do doing an interrogation of how they sometime treat the very people they are to be protecting.

From the moment that you will read this book until the time that the United States Congress act that is if they will hear my plead for justice or until the time when people of good will and those that advocate for justice on behalf of the voiceless in the society, you can rest assured that the security apparatus will come against me with everything they got; well again it's a while now since they were instructed to collect every bit of information on me and report where I am at every giving point. So except for the newest inventions they are already using everything they got. I am saying nothing new; all that I am saying is what they are already doing to me.

"Jungle justice: passing sentence on the equality of belligerents in non-international armed conflict"

"A special challenge posed by the international humanitarian law (IHL) principle of equality of belligerents in the context of non-international armed conflict is the capacity of armed opposition groups to pass sentences on individuals for acts related to the hostilities. Today this situation is conflated by the concurrent application of international human rights and criminal law. The fair trial provisions of IHL can incorporate their human rights equivalents either qua human rights law or by analogy, recognizing that human rights law does not account for the anomalous relationship between a state and non-state party. It is argued that the preferred solution is the latter. This would put greater focus on the actual fairness of insurgent courts rather than on their legal basis. Moreover, it would be consistent with the equality of belligerents principle, a vital condition to encourage IHL compliance by armed opposition groups."

*J. Somer – Jungle justice: passing sentence on the equality of belligerents in non-international armed Conflict (Volume 89 Number 867 September 2007)

I really did not intend to mention it but circumstance is causing me to so; is it for fear of retributions, I really don't know, but there is always a possibility of people wanting to get even. Am I a victim of jungle justice, minus the physical brutality ; considering the false allegation, spreading of false **ramous and character assassination. The emotional and physiological distress, I will let you decide.**

**Is it only in third world country that Jungle Justice exist? Maybe what's about its equality of belligerents?**

**I will devote a special section in my next book on the topic of Jungle Justice.**

# An Appeal to the United States Congress

I am appealing to these statesmen who are also watchmen on the wall—Rev. Al Sharpton, Rev. Jesse Jackson, and other people of goodwill—to please hear my cry for justice.

*To the Congress of the United States of America, integrity of character is all that one holds on to when all else is lost. Obtaining it is a process, sustaining it is a delicate task, destroying it is inconceivable. For so many nobles have fallen short of its grace when foolishness overpowers wisdom, to which your honorable membership is of no exception. Robbing the innocent of it is not a choice of theirs but that of men with the motive of greed.*

Let the words of Mordecai resonate with you as you contemplate on your cores of actions: *"And who knoweth whether thou art come to the kingdom (Congress) for such a time as this?"*

I will climax this book with an early morning vision. It was in the month of June, not long after I commenced the writing of this book. I started a monthlong fasting and prayer, and it came to pass that on Saturday night, the sixteenth of June 2012, I prayed from 12:00 midnight to 1:45 a.m.

I turned off the light and lay in bed to sleep. At 5:00 a.m., my alarm sounded off. I awoke and turned off the alarm. I remained lying in bed and began to pray in my heart. I don't know how long I had been praying, but I found myself in a movie hall. Everyone were checked, and we sat down to watch the movies. In the movies, there was a war taking place. So many people lost their lives and others had no food to eat.

I then saw the Rev. Billy Graham, not preaching, but just talking and telling the people about Christ. He was saying that war was not the answer, but Christ was the answer. As the movies continued, there was a man sitting next to me. He doubted everything that Rev. Billy Graham was saying about Christ being the answer. I turned my attention to the man and began to administer to him about heaven. Just then I died. I knew to myself that I was dead. As I closed my eyes in death, I opened my eyes in heaven.

As I opened my eyes, the Lord Jesus Christ was standing right in front of me. He called my name three times, "Emmett, Emmett, Emmett." He then acknowledged that I am a pastor and said to me, "I have a crown for you but Brother Onesimus, in the church will have to come and testify, after which I will give you your crown."

While awaiting Brother Onesimus, many other people were being called on the stage. One by one, they came and one by one he gave them their crown. While still waiting for Brother Onesimus, everything started getting dull. The duller things got I felt myself back on my bed. This took place on Sunday morning, June 17, 2012.

I mentioned in the vision of closing my eyes in death and opening it in heaven. This is what the word of God is saying: *"For we walk by faith, not by sight: We are confident, I say and willing rather to be absent from the body, and to be present with the Lord. Wherefore we labour, that whether present or absent, we may be accepted of him"* (2 Corinthians 5:7-8).

The DHS has done its damage to me. Apart from Christ in me, which is my hope of glory, physically I am dead. What the DHS is now waiting for is my burial to take place.

## THE END

www.ingramcontent.com/pod-product-compliance
Lightning Source LLC
Chambersburg PA
CBHW030343290526
45785CB00004B/1580